WHY MEN DON'T HAVE A CLUE

BY

JAN KING

Published by

CCC Publications
1111 Rancho Conejo Blvd.
Suites 411 & 412
Newbury Park, CA 91320

Manufactured in the United States of America

Cover ©1995 CCC Publications

Cover/Interior production by Oasis Graphics

ISBN: 0-918259-86-X

If your local U.S. bookstore is out of stock, copies of this book may be
obtained by mailing check or money order for $7.99 per book (plus
$3.00 to cover postage and handling) to: CCC Publications; 1111
Rancho Conejo Blvd.; Suites 411 & 412; Newbury Park, CA 91320.

Pre-publication Edition – 6/95

DEDICATION

*To my dear friends Bill and Roberta Isgreen
who have been a constant source of
personal and professional support—
my love and thanks*

ACKNOWLEDGEMENTS

I would like to thank all the women who took the time and effort to share their thoughts with me about why men are clueless. Obviously, I couldn't have written this book without their help. I also want to thank the women who contributed their witty comments to the "Classic Clueless Quips" section. Among them are, Yvonne Bracy, Margaret Herrmann, Susan German, and Caroline O'Connell.

And I would like to send my heartfelt thanks to Ann Landers, the brilliant columnist, for providing me with words of encouragement and support throughout the years. Even before my first book was published, she took the time to pen a note to me telling me I had "talent" and to "keep at it." And those words coming from a professional of her stature to a struggling housewife-cum-author have sustained me through ten books and will never be forgotten.

Also, I want to thank my editor, Cliff Carle, who went way beyond the call of duty in terms of time and input in helping to organize, collate, and present the information gathered for this book in a most coherent and readable format.

And, as always, to my husband and publisher, Mark, all my love and gratitude for your unwavering support in everything I do.

CONTENTS

INTRODUCTION

Every woman alive has experienced an exasperating argument with her spouse which ended up with her shaking her head in disbelief and saying, "The man doesn't have a CLUE what I'm talking about!"

This is a book which talks woman to woman about very common problems we've all experienced with our husbands or boyfriends at various times during our relationships. Some of the issues may be things you are facing now, or will be facing in the future. I sent hundreds of surveys to women all over the country (some of the women I knew personally and others I've never met) and asked them to relate their personal stories in which they found their spouse or significant other to be totally "clueless." I gave them a scenario to read in which a husband and wife had a difference of opinion. It clearly demonstrated that the man had no idea of where the wife was "coming from." I asked these women to tell me about any experience (serious or funny) with their husband or partner in which they felt he exhibited truly "clueless behavior." I've also talked to a great deal of women of all ages to learn about their most frequently encountered relationship problems. Then I assembled my findings in the form of scenarios. Some are direct quotes from the women who responded to my surveys, while others are paraphrased accounts.

As an author of eight books dealing with female problems and interaction between the sexes, I have been invited to appear on many television talk shows in the capacity of a "relationship expert," giving advice to women who are experiencing problems with their spouses. Although it is impossible to learn everything about relationships and their inherent problems in the limited amount of allotted TV time or from a brief letter, I draw upon the common experiences of all couples when forming conclusions. Many of these problems share similar origins and follow the same destructive patterns when left unresolved.

When women talk with other women, the most frequently discussed topics are problems with their kids, their hormonal difficulties, and conflicts with their husbands or boyfriends. This book is about the way men often react to these problems with negativity or with complete denial. In today's society, when women complain about men, it's referred to as "male bashing." Okay, it's a cute and topical phrase, but it's really not what we're doing here. What men don't understand is that the process of discussing our "men" problems with our girlfriends not only makes us feel better, but it allows us to become a lot MORE tolerant of their behavior. In effect, women have always acted as other women's psychiatrists. This is the nature of relationships between women. This shouldn't threaten men because it actually works to their adva tage. In most cases, (unless the problems are of an extremely abusive nature), women will counsel other women in methods of learning to cope more successfully with their marital or dating problems. And the ultimate goal is to preserve their relationships while preserving their sanity at the same time.

It is unfortunate that the term "male bashing" has gained so much popularity. It scares men to death—and rightfully so. Many men feel that women get together and ridicule them, making them appear weak in the other woman's eyes. This is not the intent of this book. But I do handle things with a great deal of humor, because I feel that it really puts a lot of these problems in their proper perspective. I think that most relationships could use a good dose of humor. Perhaps the lack of it underlies many of the problems between men and women today. We take ourselves SOOOOO seriously nowadays. In many ways, we have become such a "politically correct" society, we've lost the ability to laugh at ourselves.

Also, you're probably going to be surprised to find out that women are sometimes an equal part of the problem. Admittedly, women do give off "mixed signals" which confuse men. Remember, no one gender can always be "right" or "wrong." As long as their are relationships between two people, there are going to be two points of view injected into those relationships.

So read, relate, and hopefully laugh while gaining some new perspectives. Then you can revisit those problems armed with some new knowledge that will allow you to cope more successfully and perhaps even solve many of them.

The Sexually Clueless

THE CLUE TO GREAT SEX

As I stated in the Introduction, prior to writing this book, I sent out hundreds of surveys asking women to write about one or several situations in which they found their man to be totally "clueless." These situations were about instances where women felt that men had a total lack of understanding of a problem and would never be able to see it from the woman's point of view. In the majority of the surveys I received for this book, the area that women found men to be most "clueless" was about sex. They complained about men's insensitivity to women's feelings and their lack of knowledge, in general, about how to make love to a woman. The women who answered the surveys felt that most men were unwilling to discuss their problems concerning sex with women, because men were convinced they knew everything about it already. And that's the problem in a nutshell—pun intended. Guys seem to be of the opinion that if a woman is turned off to sex, it's because SHE'S FRIGID. However, if she appears oversexed at a particular moment when he isn't, she's "acting like a slut." If she is struggling with a problem and seems preoccupied, he feels all she needs is to "get laid" and everything will be okay again. When will men ever "get it?" The answer lies in the approach. Women want to be ROMANCED. We want tenderness, affection, and a man's undivided attention. We want to feel like a man is giving something TO us, not just taking FROM us. It's really so simple. If men just took the time to ask US what turns us on, we WOULDN'T be so turned off.

1

Scenarios dealing with sexual interactions between men and women appeared most frequently in the surveys women answered. Most women have probably experienced one or more of the same situations. You should be able to gain a better understanding of the origins of the problems when you read the paragraphs which analyze what's really motivating the people involved in the scenario. And then, hopefully, you'll be able to apply the advice given to your own relationship problems and be able to formulate an equitable compromise or permanent solution for them.

#1 WILL SEX END THE BATTLE?

The Scenario:

You and your man have just had one of the most horrendous "knock-down-drag-out-fights" of your life. We're not talking about the actual physical kind (although in some instances this applies too), rather the nasty, verbally abusive kind where you have called each other every rotten name that comes to mind. You have told each other why you hate them in about 50 different ways, and if you know a second language you've thrown in those insults too. The fight has ended with no resolution, lots of bitterness, and a pile of kleenex. As you are sitting on the bed filled with HATE AND RAGE, he decides that everything will be hunky-dory again if you just make love. And with this in mind, he makes his move.

Your body tenses like a week-old corpse and becomes just as cold. And you're thinking, "Is this man out of his bleepin' mind or what?? He has got to be the sickest puppy on the planet. I HATE THIS—I HATE HIM. At this moment, all I want to do is KILL this S.O.B. not SCREW him!"

So what do you do now? Nine times out of ten, you will submit rather than start another Viet Nam experience where everyone ends up a loser. You know in your heart that if you still act steamed, it's going to lead to more ugly words and more ugly looks from his face. So while you're making "love" (and I use the term in the loosest context possible) you are fantasizing about grabbing Sharon Stone's ice pick and hacking him to bits. You fantasize that you are Lorena Bobbitt and will teach him a lesson about the true meaning of taking a "short cut." And while you are wrestling with your rage, you are scratching his back to keep yourself from disemboweling him. And all the while the "clueless one" is thinking... "Wow!! There's nothing like a great fight to turn a woman on!!"

Am I right? Why do men feel that a good roll in the hay cures everything, and you're back to 'square one' again? What men don't have a clue about is:

a. You're still festering with anger and building additional resentment.

b. You're disgusted with yourself for submitting to him.

c. You're disgusted with his insensitivity.

d. You're seriously contemplating using that Ginsu knife.

Well, maybe not all of the above, but 3 out of 4 ain't bad.

PERPETUATING THE PROBLEM

To cover all bases, let's backtrack. There are some women who have said that when they did submit to sex while still angry, their anger worked FOR them. They found that the roll in the hay turned into a very passionate experience and they actually forgot about the fight that preceded it. If this was the case, great—there is no problem. However, it's impossible to predict beforehand if your anger will be able to work positively for you. In MOST instances, this isn't what happens.

The basic difference in the way men and women approach the sex act happens in the MIND. And a good number of men don't like to get into long discussions with their spouses, because they aren't as proficient in their communicative skills. Their way of "making-up" instead, is to have sex as a "quick-fix." But if you don't want to have sex, you're going to have to be strong and honest enough to say so. By reluctantly submitting, you're going to carry your hurt and anger through the sex act right into the next day. You'll be silent, sulky and distant. Or you might be hostile and bitchy. Everyone reacts in a different way. But the fact remains that the man is going to be even more clueless about what's going on with you the next day, IF YOU DON'T TELL HIM HOW YOU FEEL. What you have done is sent him a CONFLICTING SIGNAL, and it's no wonder he doesn't understand the way you're acting.

SO WHAT'S THE BEST WAY TO HANDLE IT?

It's up to the woman to "clue" him in. You have got to tell the man that you're still angry, and in your mind the argument hasn't been resolved. Assure him that you still love him, but right now you are definitely not in the right frame of mind to make love. Tell him that you need a night's sleep to think things over and tomorrow you'll be a lot calmer and ready to discuss the problem more rationally. Even though at this moment you feel like shouting in his face "Are you kidding, you bum? I'd rather have sex with the dog," you need to realize that will not be the way to accomplish anything—it will only keep your tempers flaring. It's not easy to do, but the wisest approach is the softer approach of saying something like this:

"Honey, making love now would be a negative experience for me. I'm still angry and hurt. It would be unfair to both of us for me to fake the feelings it takes to make love. It would be a dishonest and empty act and one I'm sure you wouldn't enjoy very much either. I would really appreciate your respecting my feelings about this."

After a good night's sleep, you should be able to discuss the problem more calmly until it has been resolved to both your satisfactions. Then you can put it past you and resume your relationship in an environment of better communication.

#2 FOND O' FONDLING

The Scenario:

"My husband and I were out for a special evening at a very fancy restaurant. Just as we were entering the dining room with the maitre d' leading the way, he playfully pinched my rear in front of everyone. I think that in some twisted way, he thought he was flattering me. He didn't have a clue that I felt like returning the gesture by grabbing his crotch until his knees buckled and he fell to the floor. At that moment, he made me feel like I should be dressed in red spandex, fishnet stockings, flashing cleavage, and wearing a price tag saying '$100 per hour.'"

WHY MEN DO THIS

What is acceptable as playful affection is vastly different between couples. There are some women who would take this pinch as a compliment, giggle, and feel flattered. But most will not. Most women will interpret this action as insulting and inappropriate, because they feel it makes them look cheap.

So why doesn't the guy see it this way? Probably because he is still behaving in the same manner that he did in high school. And this is his immature way of paying her a compliment. Let's face it, this kind of behavior usually comes from men who haven't been enlightened in their ideas about what women find flattering. Also, it's an act of showing possession which serves to stroke his own ego. The act of touching a woman in a sexual way in public is done to make the statement:

"This babe belongs to me and me alone. She is crazy about me, and loves it when I put my hands on her."

HOW TO RE-EDUCATE YOUR MAN

This is a tricky proposition. If you feel that your man behaves this way because he honestly feels it's flattering to you, then you need to respond with kindness and without condescension. Preaching will only turn him off and he'll immediately become defensive and turn a deaf ear to your suggestions. The best way to get your point across is to first talk to him in private. When you're alone, sit down and explain to him that it is very important to you that you receive treatment that is respectful. Tell him that you realize he is acting out of love, but you both obviously have different feelings about what constitutes respectful displays of affection. And as a grown woman and mother (if you are one), fondling you in public is embarrassing to you, because you feel it demeans who you are. Tell him you love his attention and sexual playfulness, but to please reserve that more intimate behavior for times when you are alone with him. Then you'll be able to gladly return his affection, and you can BOTH enjoy the moment.

You will need to spell out what YOU FEEL is appropriate behavior in public. It may be a little kiss on the cheek or holding hands—whatever you are COMFORTABLE with. It varies a great deal in women. But after you have set the limits, you have to be consistent. Once you've explained your position, don't turn around and get annoyed at him if there is a time you want more affection in public. He's not a mind reader. You have to be reasonable and remember you can't have it both ways.

#3 TIMING IS EVERYTHING

The Scenario:

You've had an incredibly hectic day. The kids were sick and screaming. You're running from one errand to the next, you've made dinner for the family, done three loads of laundry, taken care of paying the bills, and then dragged yourself up to bed at midnight. You showered, fell into bed totally exhausted and happily sank your head into the pillow. Within minutes, like clockwork, you feel the old familiar tap on your shoulder.... and hear those DREADED words... "Honey, Mr. Weenie is lonely and needs some attention."

Here's what you REALLY FEEL LIKE DOING:

    a. put a sock on Mr. Weenie and suffocate him
    b. show Mr. Weenie what happened to Mr. Bobbitt
    c. tell Mr. Weenie to start (and finish) without you

THE CLASSIC DILEMMA

Okay, I'm responding to this dilemma with humor. After all, he only wants to make love to you—not beat you up. However, in your exhausted state they seem to be the same thing. Most women find it a dilemma because they do not want their mate to feel rejected or insulted—which men will in 99% of the cases. So your conscience tells you to say "yes," but your body says that the energy it would take to have an orgasm could kill you. And you know that there isn't going to be any foreseeable change in this ongoing situation. As long as there are the kids, the killer days, and no chauffeur or nanny magically appearing to give relief...guess what? You're stuck.

Why do men's biological clocks make them crave sex after midnight or at six in the morning? Why are they clueless that these are absolutely the WORST times for a woman with kids and responsibilities? You would think that after several years of trying to make love to a comatose woman they'd get the hint and change their game plan.

WHAT THE GUYS HAVE TO SAY

"It doesn't matter if I approach her at midnight, at 6 A.M. or anytime in between, she's NEVER in the mood."

IF IT'S NEVER A GOOD TIME

Okay gals, let's get real honest. Is there any truth to what these men are saying? In many cases, women may have to admit there is validity. So now you'll have to think about why you're becoming a lot less sexual than you used to be. Yes, it is true that a day of whining kids, solving everybody's problems, dirty clothes and dishes does not foster a self-image of being a sexual bombshell. But remember, you love him, and you do not want your relationship to evolve into sexual apathy. And it is EASY to get there. You give and give all day long. And at the end of the day, curling up in bed with a great book and enjoying some much needed solitude does seem a lot more desirable than rolling around the sheets working up a sweat. This is understandable. But there has to be a compromise somewhere, or else your relationship will begin to suffer under these conditions.

SO HOW DO I CHANGE THINGS?

 THE WIN-WIN APPROACH:

There are no pat answers. You've heard it before, but now it's time to put the advice into ACTION. Couples need to MAKE TIME for themselves and their sex life. Sex will always be a crucial part of your relationship and should never be pushed down in importance to the last thing on your list. If midnight is always going to be a time when you are exhausted, then you need to find an acceptable alternative time. Put the kids to bed earlier, skip the chores, and use the extra hour you've created to make love. You will need to change your priorities to a point where it is MORE IMPORTANT to make love with your husband than getting the laundry or other chores done at a particular time. You can always put off doing the laundry or dusting or waxing the floor without it damaging your marriage. But you cannot continually put off making love without damaging your marriage. So hire a sitter, go out on the weekends, and come home relaxed and in the proper mood to make love. Or hire a sitter to take the kids to the movies while you stay home and enjoy quality time with your husband. Yes, it takes planning and adjusting your schedule. When the old way isn't working for you, then you are going to have to make a change. The old adage is true, "Where there's a will, there's a way."

It is self-defeating to take the attitude that you can NEVER find time to be together. And if you persist in this way of thinking, it is going to lead to bigger marital problems. If you fall into the pattern where you've both given up, then it's time to think about counseling. Chances are there are larger problems underlying your refusal to find a solution. People who "can never find time" to make love are avoiding physical contact with their mate. And the reasons why they are doing this need to be examined by a therapist to ultimately gain resolution.

But we can certainly laugh at the simpler problems, because they are situations that pop up in any relationship. When we admit that none of us is perfect, we can lighten up about it. We women sure as heck aren't those sexual beings portrayed in R-rated movies panting and clawing at the sheets and shuddering through pouty red lips of desire. Women get tired. We go to bed wearing T-shirts half the time. We occasionally fake an orgasm to keep our husband happy. And you know what? It's okay. We all do it. But remember, the basic purpose of a relationship is to express our love to one another. It is one of the most important things we can do as a couple to keep that relationship growing. And if we find that desire is waning, we need to seek some help in finding out what is getting in our way.

#4 SAY WHAT???

The Scenario:

"I've been in a serious relationship with a man for the past few months. The other night we were in the middle of enjoying some passionate, loving, steamy foreplay. I was totally swept away by his loving words and caresses. And then, I couldn't believe my ears when he said: 'Oh God, baby...of all the breasts I've ever touched, YOURS are the softest.'

Is this the most clueless statement ever made by a man or what? I felt like I was getting punched in the face in the middle of foreplay. Where are men's brains? Don't they realize that comparing you to another woman during romantic circumstances is the biggest turnoff on Earth?"

THE INTERPRETATION

This is one of those situations in which you can be sure that women will share the same adverse reaction. After hearing those words, we'd all dry up like prunes on the spot. A typical female response would be, "Just how many breasts am I competing with...times two?"

I guess this guy has never listened to Billy Joel, who said "Just leave a tender moment alone." In his attempt to make her feel incredibly special, he made her feel like she was just one of many in his line of conquests. It's obvious that his intent was NOT to hurt her, but his insensitivity in choosing those particular words certainly did.

LONG MEMORY

What men need to be clued in on is that when it comes to words of endearment said in the bedroom, a woman's mind is like a steel trap. Whatever he says to her will remain locked in her memory for eternity. Why is that? Who knows? It ranks up there with the mysteries of the great Pyramids at Cheops and the Hanging Gardens of Babylon. But it's positively true. Statements made during lovemaking are processed and recalled for as long as she lives. And unfortunately, men are judged by them...big time. And COMPARISONS of ANY kind with other women, especially comparing intimate body parts is never going to be taken as a compliment. It's not flattering, because no matter how it's phrased, the meaning can be interpreted only one way. The man is telling her that he is thinking about <u>some other woman</u> while making love to her.

During lovemaking, a woman looks up to the man as her knight in shining armor. It's the one time all that equal rights stuff goes out the window. She wants to be ROMANCED. She wants her man to assume control and make her feel like she's the only woman alive for him. And comparing her breasts to a cast of thousands is about the most clueless remark this guy could have made under any circumstances. What women DO want to hear is anything from the heart. As long as it doesn't sound rehearsed or isn't a comparison, a loving remark will do wonders for unleashing a woman's full sexual potential, as well as her desire to please.

If you are in the same situation and it happens only one time, you probably shouldn't make a big deal over it. His intentions were good, it's just that his phrasing was a bit tacky. However, if it happens often in your interaction with him, you'll need to tell him that even though you understand he THINKS he's paying you a compliment, he's killing the romantic moment. You might put it like this: "Sweetheart, when you compare me to another woman during lovemaking, it really puts a damper on my romantic feelings. It makes me feel like you are thinking about someone else when you're making love to me. I take responsibility for interpreting it this way, but it's something I just can't seem to get past. Would you do me a favor and leave the comparisons out of the bedroom? It would make me happy and be a lot better for our relationship."

#5 TAKE A CLUE FROM THE FLU

A friend of mine told me this story a few years ago. Because I received so many scenarios similar to hers, I felt it was a must to include it.

The Scenario:

"At 6 P.M. one night I dragged myself into bed with a 103 degree temperature, chills, and muscle aches. I put on a skimpy nightie first because I was burning up with fever. When my fiancee came home, I figured I'd get some much-needed 'TLC.' I told him how miserable I felt with the headache and fever. I was flushed, my head was stopped up, and I know that I looked like hell. He sat down on the bed next to me and I expected that he would offer to get me an aspirin or a cold washrag for my forehead. Instead, I was shocked to find that what I got was his awkward attempt to engage in foreplay! In my delirium I thought, 'No—I must be mistaken.'

But when he persisted with more aggressive fondling and kissing, my worst suspicions were confirmed.I was in total disbelief. I kept thinking 'Has this guy lost his mind? I'm a couple of seconds from expiring, and he wants to GET IT ON! No matter how sick I am, he's definitely a lot 'sicker' than me.' I was so turned off by his behavior that I told him to get out of the room. This incident combined with many of his other unacceptable behaviors led to our eventual breakup."

POSSIBLE MOTIVATIONS

Boy, here's a tough one. His clueless behavior has to be rated way up there on the chart. Now granted, this doesn't occur in the greater part of the population, but it came up often enough in the surveys to include it. And you know what? I don't have a clue why this man acted so rudely. Maybe it was because that little nightie turned him on. Or maybe her state of total vulnerability turned him on. Or last but not least, maybe he was "playing doctor" and thought an injection of his own would make her feel better. Sorry, but it's easy to get flip about this one. One thing is clear. No matter what his motivation, the man was suffering from a massive case of insensitivity.

Actually, his motivation is beside the point in this scenario. My advice is simply that this woman or any other woman in the same situation has the perfect right to say "no." You should tell the man that it's not acceptable to take advantage of you when you're down....literally. Regardless of how you handle a similar situation, it doesn't take away from the fact that the man's actions show a lack of integrity. This kind of behavior is a form of abuse and should trigger a "red flag" in the minds of women who are subjected to it.

THE WIN-WIN APPROACH:

On the other hand, some women will not feel so offended in the same situation if the guy isn't being too aggressive or too insensitive. They might take a lighter view of what's happening. If this is the case for you, just say, "Hey horny guy—give me a break. If you nurse me back to health with a little tenderness and compassion, when I'm well I'll give you a 'special treat!'"

#6 BOMBING WHEN BOMBED

The Scenario:

"This is a problem that I've been going through for the past two years with my husband. We'll go to a party and start off having a great time. Then I'll

notice that he's really putting the booze away pretty good. I'll try to slow him down, but it makes him angry and he just ignores me the rest of the evening. When we get home, he invariably gets very amorous and decides it's time to make love. But he doesn't have a clue that his vital part has become anesthetized along with his brain. What's more, I get stuck putting up with his boozy breath, sloppy foreplay, and the worst yet... in his inebriated state, it will take him hours to have a climax, if at all. He doesn't have a clue about just how unattractive he is when he's drinking. If he would only take a good look at himself, maybe he would see how awful making love to a drunk can be."

WHAT MEN DON'T GET

Besides the inability to achieve a timely orgasm, men don't seem to get the fact that it's repulsive making love with a slobbering, incoherent and uncoordinated lover. In fact, it's an ordeal. Maybe if you're both inebriated it can work out because neither will get turned off. But with one partner sober and the other drunk, it's a nightmare.

Why do men turn into Romeos when they drink? In most cases, it's just a simple matter of losing their inhibitions. Many people have the first drink at home BEFORE the party, to "loosen up" for a social situation. It's logical to assume that a person must feel intimidated by any situation that they have to face with the "help" of alcohol. Maybe for some men, this goes for making love, as well.

ROMEO NEEDS A SOBERING DISCUSSION

The key here is to talk with him BEFORE this situation happens. When he's had too much to drink, it will be an exercise in futility—exactly like the sex he's trying to perform. So wait until the following day when he's sober before you sit down with him and explain your feelings. Tell him that you will simply not agree to making love when he's intoxicated. Explain that his functions are impaired and sex becomes physically undesirable as well as uncomfortable for you. Also, let him know that you find him unattractive in that condition. And even though you love him very much, you feel that making love when he is drunk is degrading to the love you have between you.

Now, you may not feel exactly this way. So use your own words, recalling how his actions make YOU feel. Remember that sex is a mutually consenting act of love. And in order to keep it that way, there needs to be boundaries. This goes for BOTH of you. If YOU are drinking too much, he will probably feel the same way about you. And his feelings must be honored, the same as yours.

Underlying the whole problem is something that I haven't mentioned. And that is that this man sounds like he's got a serious drinking problem. However, for the sake of sticking to the immediate problem addressed in the scenario, I left out a discussion about alcoholism in general. But this doesn't mean it should be overlooked. The fact of the matter is that this woman will probably never reach any satisfactory resolution with her husband until he gets help with his drinking problem. She may be able to reason with him while he's sober, but it will be forgotten the next time he's drunk. And as time goes on, she's going to suffer through many more unpleasant situations until his drinking habits change.

#7 THE ULTIMATE PLEASURE GIVER

I felt this story was so funny, I decided to include it even though it's not a "typical" problem. But it's one that is sure to give you a good chuckle for the day. The woman who wrote about it has been very happily married for nine years. And I think that her wonderful sense of humor has a great deal to do with making her relationship a very happy one.

The Scenario:

"One night my husband and I were making some very passionate love. He was getting into it, body and soul, and we were really beginning to 'rock n' roll' in our big, king-sized bed. But soon I began to realize that with each 'love thrust,' I was getting pushed closer and closer to our huge slatted oak headboard. Within seconds, my head was becoming wedged between the slats and I started to panic. I began shouting 'OOOH, OOOH, OOOW!' By now, my head was jammed far enough between the slats to cause some serious pain. But the louder I shouted the harder he went at it, thinking I was screeching in incredible pleasure.

Finally, I had to shout 'Honey—Stop it! Stop it!' Rocked out of his moment of grand passion, he abruptly stopped and yelled 'What's the matter?'

I pointed to the headboard and cried, 'My head—it's STUCK!'

At that moment, all I could envision were the giggling paramedics sawing off the headboard, and carrying me out of the house with my head wedged between the slats. But fortunately, thanks to a little Vaseline, all that happened was a few tell-tale scabs on my ears for a week and a lot of laughs between us for months after that."

THE STUFF THAT GOOD LUNCHES ARE MADE OF

There have to be thousands of stories similar to this one floating around out there in which some clueless guy interprets a woman's "yelps" to mean that he is one hell of a stud thank goodness for men's big egos. They often provide us with a lot of laughs over a girls' lunch.

CLASSIC CLUELESS QUIP:

"A man's sex drive has been compared to a microwave oven—hot, fast, and rather tasteless. A woman's is more like a crock pot—slow, tender, and juicy."

The Clue to Hormones

From the onset of our periods and continuing through menopause, women are the victims of hormonally induced behaviors ranging from mild irritability to nightmarish tirades. We have mood swings where we go from weepy to blubbering to euphoric. We can act unpredictably and not even we understand why.

It's no wonder that men are clueless about what's going on with women. Men will never be able to adequately understand hormonal problems simply because they'll never experience them firsthand. Men will never have to suffer through periods, menstrual cramps, bloating, childbirth, post-partum depression or any of it, because they were born with a Y chromosome instead of an X. This is one topic which will never fully be understood by men because they don't have the same anatomy and physiology as a woman.

So we'll need to cut men a little slack here, gals. They aren't always being "insensitive" to our problems involving hormonal interference; they just have an awfully hard time relating to them. And this part IS understandable.

Let's see what women complained about most in the hormone/PMS department.

#1 DON'T GO WITH THE FLOW

There were many women who wrote about the problems they encounter having intercourse during their period. This is a topic that all of us face, but few feel comfortable discussing, because of its intimate nature. But it's a very common one that confronts all of us once a month through several decades. Therefore, I felt that many women would be very interested in seeing how others handled problems relating to it.

15

The Scenario:

"I hate the first day of my period. I feel bloated, my breasts are killing me, I feel drained, irritable, and have little or no desire for sex. But the real problem is my husband. He always wants to make love, regardless of my time-of-the-month. All I want to do, on the other hand, is go to bed with an inanimate object—my hot water bottle. Then I realize that I have five more days to go. He tells me that if he has to wait five more days, he will explode. At that moment in time, I feel this option might be best for both of us. I wish he wouldn't be so insensitive about how I am feeling. Especially during the first few days of my period, having sex is the last thing I want to do. But if I refuse him, he gets very upset because he feels so rejected."

HOW TO DEAL WITH HIS REJECTION

Naturally, he is going to feel rejected. From his point of view, you are only having your period—you're not terminally ill. However, any woman who chooses NOT to have intercourse during her period is totally justified. Let's face facts. It's messy, uncomfortable, and for some women, it will increase their flow to a point where they are unable to continue. This is a highly individual choice depending on your physiology. Some women find it acceptable in the latter days of their cycle, some just don't want to do it until their cycle is completely finished.

Considering that the average period lasts from 2 to 7 days, it can involve a time span of up to one week a month. Some men will not want to have intercourse during this time, others will. But no matter how many days, most men feel like it's over two weeks a month of abstinence rather than just a few days.

How many times have you heard this "sensitive" remark coming from a man describing his wife?

"Oh yeah, she's got the rag on 30 days a month."

Well, it may seem like it to most men. But we can state with certainty that any woman who has her period for 30 days would not only be abstaining from sex but from much of life as well.

YOU CAN'T FIGHT NATURE BUT YOU CAN GET AROUND HER

 THE WIN-WIN APPROACH:

Keeping in mind that it's YOUR body, you have a perfect right to say no to anything which will make you feel even more uncomfortable than you are already feeling during your period. But, by the same token, he has a perfect right to feel disappointed and a bit rejected. So ladies, as soon as you're up to it—get creative! To assuage his feelings of rejection, give him a real pleasurable alternative like oral sex, or a night of kisses and caresses, or a sexy massage, or whatever else will make you both happy. You might find that after following this routine for a while, he actually begins to LOOK FORWARD to your time of the month!

#2 CLUES FROM THE BLUES

The Scenario:

"I get into weepy blue funks just prior to my period. One day, standing in my bedroom trying unsuccessfully to zip up my tight jeans over my bloated belly, I was becoming more disgusted by the minute. I knew I was bloated and I also knew that I had gained five extra pounds. My husband walked in and saw me struggling with the zipper. And he 'innocently' remarked, 'Getting a paunch there, hon? YOU should work out with Kathy. Five kids and she still has the tight belly of a teenager!'

With that, I burst into tears and told him he had about as much sensitivity as a rock. He got angry and stomped off muttering about how 'impossible' I was becoming."

DID SHE OVER-REACT?

Only one answer here. Is the Pope Catholic? Come on, admit it! She did. Why? Because deep down, she knew she needed to get rid of those five extra pounds that were making her miserable. And he touched that sore spot in her. Maybe if she wasn't in such a hormonal funk, she would have shrugged it off.

WAS HE BEING INSENSITIVE?

Damn right he was. Men have got to learn that comparisons with another woman are not only hurtful, but they're unfair, too. You are who you are—and you should not have to worry about competing with Kathy's belly or anybody else's body parts for that matter.

THE WIN-WIN APPROACH:
I think that the best course of action for women in this situation would be as follows: when you have calmed down and collected yourself, you should tell him exactly what was going on inside you. You might say something like... "I know you didn't mean to hurt me with what you said, but you did. I'm having a lot of pre-menstrual tension, and I feel lousy about myself and my weight. And your remark just put me over the edge. However, it HAS made me realize that I need to diet and exercise more, because it's important that I look and feel as good as I can about myself."

Then you should give him a big smooch—and hit him up for the $300 bucks to join a health club. This makes you a winner on two counts. Not only will you get your point across without rancor, but it will be pretty darn hard for him to refuse the health club membership after he's insulted you. Now—isn't this the SMART way to handle it?

#3 WHY HE'S ACTING LIKE A <u>BOOB</u> WHEN YOU WANT <u>THEM</u>

The Scenario:

"After nursing our third child, my boobs had been sucked from their original C cup down to an A. It made me feel unattractive and inadequate in clothes—especially in my bathing suit. I began to compare myself to those jiggly gals you see everywhere, and my flat boobs were making me feel terribly depressed with myself. So I made the decision to have breast implants.

I told my husband thinking that he would love having big, perky boobs to snuggle up against every night. Instead, he hit the roof! He gave me a bunch of reasons that didn't make any sense. He said, 'Are you crazy?? Those things are dangerous, they could explode inside of you. Why the hell would you want to have a pair of tits hanging out like some hooker?'

I tried to explain that he used to love it when I had big breasts. Besides, I wanted to look sexy and feel good about myself again. He said, 'You are the mother of three kids. You don't need to be sexy. I think you're sexy and that should be good enough for you.' He just couldn't understand that I needed to do this for my own self-esteem. He didn't have a clue how important this was to me."

THERE'S MORE THAN MEETS THE EYE HERE

Okay, so let's analyze what this husband was REALLY saying. Why do you think he was so dead set against his wife getting implants? He loves big boobs. He probably drools over Playboy and can't wait to see "Baywatch" every week. But think about what he said to her.

"You're a mother and don't need to be sexy." You've got it!! He feels THREATENED. And that's what's underneath all his anger. He interprets her desire for bigger breasts as a sign that she's discontented with her role as a wife and mother. All he can think of is the threatening "statement" that she wants to be SEXIER. And he must feel that "being sexy" means she's going to be flashing those new, big boobs at other men. Sure, most men want their wives to look good—but not TOO good. He sees her as wanting to develop a new sexy persona and that brings out a lot of insecurity in him.

HOW TO CONVINCE HIM

Most men will never admit that they feel threatened. They will give you a million reasons why you shouldn't get implants—some having merit like the health risks, others truly insane like you must want to look like a hooker. But the important thing in this dilemma is NOT to try and get him to admit he's feeling threatened. Rather, you need to convince him that you'll remain the same loving wife and mother you've always been regardless of your breast size. You should try to make him understand that you miss having the curves you used to have and it's making you very unhappy with yourself.

 THE WIN-WIN APPROACH:

Then tell him how the change will benefit HIM too. Men really want to hear about that. When you talk about me, me, me, it's a turnoff to them. They will feel shut out. It's only natural that a man wants to know how a change will benefit him too. So perk up his interest by saying something like: "You know honey, once I have a more voluptuous body, I'm going to feel a lot sexier for YOU. I know I'll feel more enthusiastic about making love to you because you'll be excited by my new, sexier body." Then drop it for a while. Let him get used to the idea. When you bring the subject up again, make him feel like he is a PART of the decision this time. In many cases, once the man feels more secure about the fact that you won't become more distant and he will have more fun with you, he will agree.

AND WHAT IF HE DOESN'T?.....

Then you have a decision to make. Keeping in mind that your relationship is the most important element in this picture, you're going to have to decide if the boobs are worth the rift they're going to cause. It may come down to a power struggle. You might do it anyway and find he actually loves them. Or he may harbor a long-term resentment against you for going against his wishes. Only each individual in each relationship can surmise what their spouses' ultimate reactions might be. But remember, it's one you BOTH have to live with—so think about it long and hard. If it's going to be a bone of contention for years to come, is it worth undermining your relationship?

#4 MENOPAUSAL MISERY

The Scenario:

"My husband and I are in our early fifties. Our sex life has always been very good over the years. But recently we had a night when we were about to get 'it on,' and he couldn't get 'it in.' He tried to handle the situation with humor by saying 'Honey, did you put a clamp on it? I couldn't believe what was happening. I had never gone completely dry in all the years we had been married. My vaginal muscles seemed to shut down like a vise. Naturally, I did not share his sense of humor about the whole thing. We were unable to continue making love and I broke down in tears, feeling like a failure.

Then, I guess his insecurity took over because he said, 'Was it me? Don't you find me exciting anymore?' This made me feel worse than ever, and we were both at a loss about what happened."

WHAT DID HAPPEN

Okay girlfriend, you can relax now. You have just experienced something called "vaginal dryness"—a common symptom accompanying the onset of menopause. You're also going to notice that there will be times when you try to insert a junior tampax and wonder if you're using a junior size brillo pad instead. But the real culprit is the decrease in estrogen which is making your vaginal canal dry. Granted, it's not the most pleasant thing on earth, but it's a physiological fact of life you'll be dealing with from now on. However, it does not have to force your sex life to come to a screeching halt. There are some simple, remedial steps you can take to put everything back to normal again.

THE LUBE JOB—GYN STYLE

The first thing to do is make an appointment with your gynecologist for an exam. You'll probably find out that you are going through "peri-menopause" which is the onset of the whole process of menopause. Menopause doesn't just happen in the course of a few months. It can take five or more years from start to finish. The gynecologist might do a simple blood test to determine your FSH level and see how close you are to the end of menopause. This test will determine when you have stopped ovulation, and hence will stop having periods.

The doctor might recommend E.R.T. (estrogen replacement therapy). This will lessen the symptoms of hot flashes, vaginal dryness, and other related annoyances. Or perhaps the doctor will simply recommend using a vaginal lubricant like Astroglide to reduce the friction and ease the problem. Now, it's natural for you to feel a little reluctant about having to use this aid. You will probably feel like an old 1964 Chevy that needs a "lube job." But what the hell gals, you hated the old diaphragm too—but you got used to it. Besides, women of all ages report that it seems to enhance their sensation during intercourse and use it regularly.

EDUCATING HIM ABOUT YOU

Now that you are no longer clueless, it's necessary to clue him in. We're living in an age where female problems are not discussed behind closed doors anymore. Men need to know what's going on with their spouses or girlfriends—physiologically as well as psychologically. Once he understands why it happened he will be relieved to know it had nothing to do with his performance. And we all know that where sexual dysfunction is involved, it's NEVER the man's fault—right??

#5 CRY ME A RIVER

The Scenario:

"I have never been a depressed or tearful person. But I notice that as I get older, I'm becoming prone to crying jags for the most insignificant reasons. My husband considers my behavior to be 'annoying' and never fails to point out that I am embarrassing him with my 'slobbering.' His attitude makes me furious. I've told him, 'Just who am I hurting by showing some emotion? Maybe it would do YOU some good to show a little emotion once in a while.'

Although he lacks sensitivity, I keep wondering if there is something wrong with me. I don't make a conscious decision to cry over little things, it just happens that way."

CRYING ON CUE

We need to give our men a lot more education about the role hormones play in making us blue and weepy. And it IS a fact, that these hormone problems (i.e. PMS) happen. Just before our periods, we do experience a true susceptibility to crying over things that normally wouldn't bother us. If this is happening to you, it's very important to consciously tune into your cycle and watch carefully for these blue periods.

For example, I have always been aware that just one day prior to getting my period, my whole psyche bottoms out. It's during that time that I begin to miss my two college-aged sons with a vengeance. I get really weepy thinking about how much I'd love to have them back home as little boys again. But within a day or two, the weepiness passes. Then I move forward again and become happy in the knowledge that they are healthy, growing young men, making productive adult lives for themselves. These mood swings are normal. Most women experience scenarios very similar to mine. At some point in our lives, we all go through it.

WHAT'S NOT NORMAL

Almost all of us get teary upon hearing a rousing rendition of the 'Star Spangled Banner' or watching our kid play the head cabbage in his school play. But if crying jags and general depression become frequent enough to interfere with our day-to-day functioning and they don't seem to be associated with the menstrual cycle, this is NOT "normal." This is when you'll have to dig a lot deeper to try and ascertain the underlying reasons for your continued unhappiness.

Be honest with yourself. Are you doing it only in your mate's presence to get his attention? Could your relationship with your spouse be the underlying root of your unhappiness? Are the crying spells escalating and accompanied by depression that is becoming harder and harder to shake off? Are you crying publicly as a signal that you are in need of some help? Are you beginning to feel like everyday events are getting totally out of your control? These are symptoms of some deeper and possibly much more serious problems. It could be the onset of a true depressive state which needs medication and/or counseling. Or there could be an undetected physical problem which is causing the behavior.

At this point your mate may react with a lot of anger. He might even threaten you with "shape up, or else!" His inappropriate reaction is because he's AFRAID of what's happening to you. Sure, he's exhibiting clueless behavior in handling it, but he's scared and feels helpless. Fear is a normal reaction to the unknown. This is in no way, however, excusing his behavior. In fact, it's the worst way to handle the problem.

But true emotional illness is a scary thing for everyone involved. It's not only frightening to the person suffering with it but also for those who love you and will have to cope with the problems it creates. This is why denial is the most common reaction to mental problems. Many times loved ones just pretend the problem doesn't exist because they're afraid that the long road to recovery may be too much for them to handle. But with any problem, including physical or emotional illness, IGNORING IT WON'T MAKE IT GO AWAY— ever. The sooner you get some kind of treatment, the sooner you can start becoming whole again. Too many of us, especially men, think that getting counseling is a sign of weakness. Many people feel they should be able to work through a problem of any magnitude alone. But the truth is that most of the time we can't. We can no more heal a serious physical illness without professional help than we can an emotional one.

IT IS VITALLY IMPORTANT FOR BOTH MEN AND WOMEN TO NEVER CONSIDER IT SHAMEFUL TO SEEK HELP FOR AN EMOTIONAL ILLNESS. PROFESSIONAL COUNSELING WILL NOT ONLY HELP YOUR RELATIONSHIP BUT MAY ULTIMATELY SAVE YOUR LIFE.

CLASSIC CLUELESS QUIP

"When a woman's pants get tight, she admits that she must be putting on a few pounds. A man, on the other hand, claims his pants must have shrunk."

Clueless Control Freaks

WHEN CONTROL BECOMES AN ISSUE

The issue of control arises constantly in relationships. Historically, there has been an ongoing power struggle between the sexes. However, we hear a lot more about it in our current times as women are attempting to gain more control over their own lives. Also, men and women get stuck in behavior patterns in which they believe that exercising control over the other person will bring more control into their own lives. It is this common error in thinking that leads many couples into constant disagreements and ensuing battles.

In our parents' and grandparents' generation there were unwritten rules which governed relationships. It was a "given" that women were supposed to stay home and raise the children. They were out of the work force for years and became totally dependant on their husbands for financial support. And many men liked this arrangement. They were in control and were content to keep the women "at home in their place." Remember the old adage "barefoot and pregnant?" Well, there's a lot of men who still believe in this philosophy as a way of maintaining control. But what they fail to understand is that many women who are stuck at home with very little power or freedom are unhappy women and are, in turn, contributing to an unhappy marriage.

Our present economic times have forced a lot of changes. Many women have to work because one salary isn't enough to provide adequately for the family. However, their income brings another factor into the equation. It puts them in a much better position to demand their right to have an equal voice

25

in the decision making within the family. The economic nature of marriage is changing and men are becoming more threatened.

#1 WORKING TOWARDS FREEDOM

The Scenario:

"Our youngest child has just started elementary school. Now that my days are free, I have become restless about filling my time meaningfully. My husband and I have a good marriage and although we are not poor, his salary just barely covers our basic needs. So if I went to work, the added money would be great for all those extras the whole family could use.

I told my husband, 'Honey, I've decided it would really help all of us if I go back to work. The kids are all in school, and I could work from 9 until 3 without disrupting anyone's schedule. We could all use the extra money. Besides, I feel that being more productive would make me a lot happier.'

His reaction wasn't at all what I expected. He said 'What the hell are you TALKING about? You don't need to work. You need to stay home and take care of your family. We're doing all right financially. What's your problem? Don't you want to be a wife and mother anymore?'

How could he jump to the conclusion that my wanting to work is a sign that I want to abandon my role as a wife and mother? His reaction is beyond clueless—it's just plain ridiculous!"

ARE WE ON THE SAME PLANET HERE?

I agree with her. She simply stated that she wanted to go to WORK—not break up the family or hit the streets. So we're all wondering the same thing—WHAT IN THE HELL IS HE TALKING ABOUT?

We need to really TUNE IN to what he's saying for insight as to how he's interpreting her words. It's clear from his statement, 'Don't you want to be a wife and mother anymore?' that he is interpreting her desire to work as a sign of unhappiness with her present status. He may even be afraid she's going to work in hopes of meeting another man. Sure that sounds ridiculous to us, but I believe it's one of the basic fears motivating all his anger. Another possibility is that he's also struggling with the issue of losing control. Once she is earning money, things will change in the power arena. She might not be making big bucks, but she'll gain a taste of personal as well as financial independence. And this scares him because it will undermine his current position of being in total control.

This is especially true in relationships where the woman hasn't worked before during the marriage. He has nothing to fall back on in terms of projecting what life will be like with a working wife. It's a big change. He might feel that she will have less time for the kids. He will certainly feel like she will have less time for him. I can't tell you how many marriages I know of where the women would like to work but the hell they would have to go through getting their husbands' approval keeps them from ever doing it. So they remain stuck at home—usually discontented and bitter.

WHAT MEN NEED TO BE CLUED IN ABOUT

Most women know that if their relationship is on "solid ground," then her seeking personal fulfillment through a career won't be a threat to it. Instead, they feel it will serve to make it BETTER. When we feel good about ourselves, we will bring a lot more joy and contentment into the lives of everyone we touch. Men have simply got to understand that for a great many women, in addition to being a housewife and mother, they need something more to make them feel intellectually stimulated and fulfilled. Nowadays, women are in positions such as executives, lawyers, doctors, bankers, stockbrokers, etc. Once the kids are in school, staying home, cooking, shopping, and watching Daytime TV is not going to completely fulfill them anymore. Many of us have college degrees or other training, and we want to use our skills. Or even if we don't hold lofty degrees, many women are talented writers, artists, and craftspeople who could build an exciting career utilizing those God-given talents.

Men need to understand that an unhappy, unfulfilled woman who feels stuck at home is much more likely to leave a marriage than one who is productive and feels a true sense of self-worth.

DIGGING DEEPER

If this work issue becomes a crucial factor in the survival of a marriage, then the marriage itself needs a good examination. The marriage may be floundering because the man is so controlling. Or the marriage may be in trouble for a myriad of other reasons. When the work issue arises in a troubled marriage, it just adds more fuel to his fear that she'll gain the financial independence she needs to LEAVE him. If this is the situation, then counseling is vital to repair the basic problems existing in the marriage. If they are allowed to go on unresolved, a woman may, indeed, go to work to escape the unhappiness at home. And she may find another man, realizing his worst fears. On the other hand, she may remain home and find another man, too. The point is that her employment or non-employment won't be the cause of an affair. It's the unresolved relationship problems that both of them must make their priority.

Many men are of the mind that once a woman earns her own money, she may get "uppity" and put up with a lot less. The bad news for him is this is often true. And the truth may be that she IS putting up with a lot of crap that she shouldn't, because she has no power. Yes, she may stand up for her rights a lot more when she's earning her own money. So what? There may be darn good reasons. The man may be continually treating her unfairly, because he knows she has no other alternative. If this is the case, the marriage isn't a healthy one. There are a lot of issues interacting at many different levels which need to be worked through before the relationship can grow in a positive direction.

#2 MARRIAGE ON A LEASH

The Scenario:

"Last week, I was out having a terrific time lunching with a group of girlfriends. The time slipped by, and I arrived home at four o'clock instead of two o'clock which I had originally told my husband I'd be home by. The minute I got home, all hell broke loose. My phone was ringing off the hook. My mother, sister, and others called to tell me that my husband had been frantically trying to find me. I was informed to call him at his office ASAP.

No sooner had I hung up with my mother than the phone rang. It was my husband. 'Where have you been?' he shouted. I thought you were in an accident or got carjacked or something. Where the hell have you been, and what the hell have you been doing?'

I could understand him being a little concerned, if I was several hours late. However, I don't make a practice of doing this. I think he not only over-reacted, but for some crazy reason he was also 'checking up on me.'"

CONTROL REARS ITS UGLY HEAD

In Ronald Reagan's famous words, "Here we go again." Most women who have gone through this will probably agree that he didn't really believe she was dead, lying in a ditch or carjacked. What he was really afraid of was that she might be in some Motel 6, dressed in a teddy, and rolling around on a vibrating bed with some hunky lover. Okay, maybe not EXACTLY this scenario. But I think he would never have responded with such vehemence, if he truly believed she was with her girlfriends. So why didn't he just come out and accuse her if this was what he was really thinking? Because, he can still be the "good guy" if he masks his suspicions as a concern for her safety. But if he comes right out and accuses her of possible infidelity, he knows he's going to look like an idiot as well as start World War III. The wife was angry because she saw through this ruse. Why did he turn one little afternoon of fun and freedom with her girlfriends into a nightmare experience for her?

WHAT DO YOU SAY TO AN IRRATIONAL MAN?

She can go in either of two directions. Either she can get angry and stand up for herself or back down. But think about what's really underneath his accusations. He's upset because he's totally insecure about her. Why? This requires a more extensive knowledge of their relationship which we don't have. But when she addresses the immediate problem (i.e., his anger), she must keep in mind that he is feeling very threatened. His irrational fear may stem from deep inside himself and an unexpressed insecurity about their marriage. Or maybe he doesn't trust her because of some past infidelity which occurred between them. In any event, I think the best way she can handle him is to begin by not invalidating his feelings. If you find yourself in a similar situation, my advice on how to handle this type of man is given in the following suggested dialogue:

You might say, "I'm sorry you got so upset, but truthfully I don't understand your over-reaction. You knew I was going to be having lunch with my girlfriends. We were having a great time schmoozing, and time just slipped away. But I certainly see no need for you to involve my mother or friends in this. I'm an adult, and I was merely enjoying lunch—nothing more. Why are you making such an issue out of this?"

Then you should wait for his response. He may immediately back down and apologize. If so, accept his apology but make it clear that you never expect this kind of behavior from him again. If he persists in the ruse of "fearing you were in an accident" and you intuitively feel he isn't going to be honest with you, you're going to have to draw out his hidden feelings. It should be clear to you that he's attempting to manipulate you through guilt and intimidation. Then you'll have to ask him point blank what it was about your day out with the girls that was so threatening to him. You should tell him that you wonder if he was really concerned that you were in an accident, or whether the real reason was that perhaps he thought you might not have been with the "girls." Or was he annoyed at the fact that for the two hours he didn't know where you were, he had, in some sense, lost a degree of control over you?

If you're lucky, he might get around to admitting his real fear. If he does, it's time to let your anger go and try to assure him that he has no reason to worry. You may unearth some deeper feelings too. And that's good. Once these things are out in the open and he sees there is no cause for insecurity, he probably won't repeat this scenario again.

 THE WIN-WIN APPROACH:

Once you have established the underlying reasons for his overreaction, you should try and set his mind at ease. You could propose this compromise by saying: "Now that I understand the reasons why you were so upset, I will do my best to never let this situation happen again. Next time, I'll leave the number of the restaurant where I am having lunch. And if I see that time is slipping by, I promise to call and let you know where I am. And if by some unavoidable circumstance I am unable to do so, then you can call the restaurant. But I want you to promise me that you will not call anyone in my family or any of my friends to try and track me down."

But one thing remains certain. If you do not settle this issue to both your satisfactions, he will end up controlling your every move—BECAUSE YOU ALLOWED HIM TO. I know of women who actually never go out at night with their girlfriends, because their husbands won't "allow" it. Sounds positively medieval doesn't it? But it's a fact. For reasons known only to them, they have given up control over their own lives to keep their husbands feeling secure. This is not all that unusual, believe me. I hear it over and over from women of all ages. However, each woman needs to be the judge of her own situation. Maybe these women are perfectly content with the boundaries established in their marriages. If they are, so be it. It's their lives and their decision. But for other women, this situation would be totally intolerable. We're supposed to be in relationships, not in prisons. Unfortunately, some women allow the relationship to become their prison. Personally, I feel that anyone who willingly gives up their basic freedoms to another, has a big self-worth problem going on within themself. This would indicate an urgent need for personal counseling.

#4 WHAT'S GOOD FOR THE GOOSE

The Scenario:

"My husband likes to stop by the local 'action' bar after work to have a few beers a couple of nights during the week. Also, he plays poker at a friend's house one night a week. I am very much opposed to this and want him to stay home with me and the kids on week nights. He sees nothing wrong with having a couple of nights out with the boys. He refuses to compro-

mise with me on this issue, so we've had an ongoing battle about it for a few years. I have become so frustrated with the situation that recently I decided to retaliate. I have begun hiring a babysitter on the nights he's out and started going to bars with my girlfriends. He's having a fit over it. So we continue to argue unproductively over the situation, with neither of us giving in."

QUESTION: Who is "clueless" here?

ANSWER: They both are.

EQUAL RIGHTS IN THEORY

Let's talk about rights, IN THEORY, only. If a man takes a few nights a week to enjoy his "night out," then IN THEORY, there is no reason why the woman shouldn't do the same thing. It is basically unfair to deny a woman the same privileges as a man.

IN REALITY

Now let's talk about what is actually occurring in this scenario. If he was playing poker at a buddy's home or going to the Rotary Club and she was going out for an evening of bridge, THEN the situation would be equitable. But in this case, they are not. They are both going to bars, which is not a healthy situation for any marriage. Let's get real here. A "singles' bar" is not an appropriate place for married people to be frequenting. Drinking, getting drunk, and flirting are the kind of destructive behaviors that go on at these bars. They are inundated with single people looking for dates, a one night stand, or what have you. And married people who constantly "flirt" with this type of bar scene are going to eventually run into situations which are potentially marriage wrecking. You can count on it.

THE RHETORIC

Married men and women try to defend their actions by asserting they don't "do anything" at these bars. They just go to "have a few beers and relax." Whatever their assertions, the truth is that the men and women who are regularly engaged in this behavior should be asking themselves why they are doing it. And they need to answer this question honestly. People frequent bars for vastly different reasons. If any man, married or not, regularly drinks at a bar several nights a week, he most likely has an alcohol problem. It is not healthy behavior to be out drinking three or four nights a week. And if you are somebody who does, you need to get honest about why you are sitting in that bar drinking and not at home with your family. Is the alcohol more important than your family? Is your family life so distasteful that you need to avoid it several nights a week? If so, the marriage won't be able to survive for very long without immediate counseling. Are you a woman who is frequenting bars just to "get revenge" on your husband, hoping it will "teach him a lesson?" Are you hoping that your man will get tired of you being out and ultimately stop his own trips to the tavern?

Probably, for a lot of women, this is their INITIAL motivation. They are utilizing this counter-control mechanism in hopes of making their husbands realize how unfair they're acting. But this rarely gets the results you're seeking. It just doesn't work this way. Instead, what happens is an escalation of the negative behaviors and a build-up of resentment until, eventually, everybody gets hurt. She may even talk herself into thinking that a harmless dance with a man at a bar is okay, but rarely will it stop there. Each time she visits that bar, her behavior will become a little bolder. And eventually the "harmless" flirting could end up in an affair. Eventually, all her game-playing and scheming backfires right in her face, and she's stuck with one hell of a mess. This scenario is not a fantasy. It happens thousands of times every day to men and women in all walks of life.

The point is that, of course, there should be freedoms in any relationship. But the freedoms have to be appropriate to that relationship. And going to bars alone several nights a week is NOT an appropriate behavior for anybody in a committed relationship. If any man or woman wants to be out there swinging with the singles, they need to examine their conscience to see if what they really want is to be single again.

WHICH ONE DOESN'T HAVE A CLUE?

The answer is neither do. However, many men have to evolve in their thinking and accept that no woman wants a marriage where the husband is out drinking several nights a week. Men who feel it's their "inherent right" to booze it up after work because they've put in a hard day at the office are exhibiting "cave-man" type thinking. And in today's society, it's not going to cut it with 99% of the female population. But for a woman to retaliate with the same kind of behavior is equally destructive. Two wrongs never make a right. Remember that saying?

THE WIN-WIN APPROACH:
Knowing this—what now? You have your work cut out for you. One possible solution, if both parties are agreeable, is to go out TOGETHER one night a week to a restaurant or night club. Or perhaps, the hus-

band would find it exciting to meet his wife at a bar one night a week, where they could play out a harmless fantasy of her getting "picked-up" by him. Another compromise would be for her to agree to his going out for poker or softball one night a week with the guys in return for him taking her out on another night. You can get creative with your compromises, but THE MAIN THING IS THAT YOU BOTH AGREE ON WHAT TO DO AND WHAT NOT TO DO.

If he is completely opposed to any kind of compromise, then you'll need to coax him into telling you the real reason he's choosing to stay out at night and avoiding you and the family. You'll need to spell out quite clearly what his behavior is doing to your relationship. And if you tell him that it is ultimately going to destroy the relationship and he keeps on doing it, then counseling is definitely needed. Anyone who is willing to throw away a marriage or relationship in return for a few nights out at a bar doesn't want that relationship very much. And this could be the REAL root of the problem. Women need to get out of their denial, no matter how painful it may be, and find out if there is a marriage left to save.

And if the real root of the problem lies in his alcoholism which he is unable to conquer alone, he will need counseling, AA, or both. But this is a decision he must arrive at by himself. Ultimatums don't work with a true alcoholic. They need to admit that they have a problem and seek treatment of their own volition. If he doesn't seek help, you do have the option of getting support through groups like Al-Anon or private counseling. These groups work with you to help you begin changing the way you react to someone's drinking problem. Their philosophy is that usually a change in your behavior will eventually motivate the drinker to seek help for himself.

#5 WINDOW DRESSING

The Scenario:

"My husband is constantly criticizing the way I dress. He says I look like a 'tart' and a 'hooker.' He always gets jealous when he sees another man stare at my cleavage or my butt. Then he blames me and we end up fighting about it. I just can't understand why he acts this way. He always wanted me to look sexy before we got married. He used to love me in halter tops and cut off shorts. Now he wants me to dress like a nun."

TO DRESS OR UNDRESS

Oh brother! I bet there are millions of other women out there who have been through the same squabble. There's definitely a double standard going on here. Although men hate to admit it, it's true. Men love to look at other women's boobs and fannies in the malls, walking down the street, or in girly magazines. They may even point out to their wives that some particular woman in shorts and a T-shirt has a "hot body." And the fact is that when you used to dress this way, he loved it. But NOW THAT YOU'RE MARRIED, you're not supposed to look sexy anymore. This makes the woman feel stifled. Why does a man want his wife to look "un-sexy," yet he enjoys looking at all the other sexy women out there?

This is one of those problems with no easy answers. But women have got to be very honest about the style of clothing they're wearing which is upsetting him. The question of what is in "good taste" will vary drastically from one person to another. But the big picture to keep in mind is that your partner is unhappy. Let's get to the bottom of his dissatisfaction by answering these questions honestly to ascertain if he's really justified or not.

ARE you wearing clothes that are too revealing to be in good taste? Are you going to the supermarket in tight spandex tops that reveal too much bosom for daytime wear? Are your cheeks hanging out of your cut-off shorts? If so, why are you doing this? Is he not paying you enough attention? Do you feel you have to compete with the vast number of sexy women out there to keep him interested? Why is the way you dress making him feel so insecure? Are you giving HIM enough attention? Are you intentionally flaunting too much of your private stuff because you crave attention from other men?

We hear men saying the same kinds of sentiments over and over again. "She is MY wife. There is no need for her to go flaunting her body in public for every man to drool over. The attention I give her should be enough."

You need to be honest here. If you ARE going over-board on the sexy clothing issue, you need to ask yourself what is the point in making him feel insecure? Is showing off your body in public more important to you than making him feel happy and secure in the relationship? Of course it shouldn't be. But if this is the case, it's ultimately going to hurt his trust in you and undermine your relationship.

On the other hand, many times a clueless man will provoke the situation because he just can't keep his mouth shut about how "hot" other women look. It makes you feel unappreciated and unattractive. So in your own defense, you dress extra sexy to compete for his attention. Men have to learn that they can't have it both ways. They will have to realize that they are CAUSING the problem with their own insensitivity. What it all boils down to is the issue of SECURITY. Your man wants you to be sexy and attractive but not TOO sexy or TOO attractive. He is afraid that if you look too sexy, he might lose you to that army of men out there just waiting to manhandle your luscious body. Right?

THE WIN-WIN APPROACH:

So let's lighten up on this issue and do a bit of compromising. Pull up the scoop neck an inch or so and cover a little more of that cleavage. Yank the skirt down a bit. Wear a clingy curve-fitting dress that does not show cleavage. You can still look sexy without looking trampy. But in the bedroom, anything goes. The sexier the better. It's appropriate to flaunt everything you've got here. Wear those flimsy little teddies or go braless in a skimpy muscle T-shirt and thong panties. This is the proper place to fulfill your not-so-proper fantasies. But make a deal with him. Tell him you will be more than happy to tantalize him in the bedroom—IF—and this is a BIG IF—he promises to keep his mouth shut about how sexy other women look. And hold him to it. I think it won't take very long before he realizes that he's getting the best end of this deal.

#6 SPILLING YOUR GUTS AND REGRETTING IT

The Scenario:

"In the beginning of our love affair, we felt like soul-mates. We shared our innermost secrets with one another. He told me all about his previous loves and sexual relationships with complete honesty. He told me that I was so much more special and fulfilling to him than anyone he had ever been with before. I returned the closeness by telling him about previous involvements including the men I'd gone to bed with. It was cleansing and binding.

But now I find that my words have come back to haunt me. During any disagreements, he brings up my past behavior and uses it against me. I find he is becoming increasingly more jealous and suspicious, questioning my every move or motive. It's becoming very apparent that no matter what I do from now on, he doesn't trust me because of my past. Was I foolish to tell him so much?"

LOOSE LIPS SINK SHIPS

Here's the bottom line, gals. No matter how far we think that women have advanced socially in this culture, there is still a double standard working AGAINST us. Men can sleep with an army of women and it makes them more "experienced" and "sophisticated."

But if women do the same, they are called "sluts." Of course it is totally unrealistic to expect that you led a cloistered life before you met him. However, the more deeply he grows to love you, the more he wishes that you had been Mother Theresa before you met him. Unfair? You bet. But you better get used to it, because no matter how stupid it seems, THIS IS HOW IT IS. And it's going to take an evolution of several more generations, if ever, for this kind of thinking to change.

It is important to know that it isn't dishonest to NOT reveal EVERYTHING about your past loves. They are part of your past which has nothing to do with your present partner. What possible GOOD can it do either of you by telling him lurid details about past lovers? Believe me, after years of listening to other women spill their woes on this subject, it is in your best interest to let the past remain in the past—unless it has some DIRECT bearing on your relationship in the present. (For example, if you were physically abused in the past and it's affecting your intimacy with him; or if the issue of a sexually transmitted disease is involved.) Of course it would be totally unrealistic to never discuss anything about past relationships. He certainly realizes that you didn't live in a nunnery until adulthood. However, I feel that you must be cautious about what you DO reveal, and too many passionate details or graphic accounts are just not in your best interest.

This usually works both ways, too. How many times during a moment of jealousy or insecurity have you thrown the name of one of his past girlfriends back in his face? The knowledge of his past intimacies will serve no real constructive purpose in your present relationship. Rather, it will most likely act as a catalyst that erodes your security and eats away at your confidence over time.

WHEN THE CAT'S ALREADY OUT OF THE BAG

Unfortunately, once you've told him about your past there's no way on Earth you can take it back. You're not about to tell him that the sex you had with previous men was something you never enjoyed. Sorry gals, but the knowledge of past lovers you handed over to him is going to be sealed forever in his mind. Nobody enjoys a mental picture of their loved one having passionate sex with another. Then there's always the tendency for him to believe that because you've had sex with numerous partners, you MIGHT do it again. No, it's not rational thinking. However, when two people are passionately in love with other, emotional thinking usually overrides rational thinking.

 THE WIN-WIN APPROACH:

How can you resolve this situation to both your satisfactions? Well, the first thing you'll need to do is to constantly reassure him that the past remains in the past. Your only concern is for the present and future with him and you don't want your past to ruin it. If you find that you are both throwing the past in each other's faces because of insecurity, you'll need to make a pact. Discuss the fact that the past seems to be keeping you both insecure and not allowing your relationship to grow. Promise one another that never again will you bring up anyone in your past and use the knowledge against one another.

You might even make a pact that if either one of you brings up a past lover, the offending party will have to pay $10.00 on the spot. This will tend to keep you on your toes as well as creating a diversion to get off the subject. When you're truly aware of how much this behavior interferes with the growth of your relationship, you'll both take the time to stop and think before you say anything so destructive to one another again.

CLASSIC CLUELESS QUIPS

"He loves to take your picture when you are at your all time worst—like when you've wearing your old robe with your hair in rollers or when you're cleaning the garage. He says that he needed to use up the last few shots on the roll. Then he shows them to EVERYONE."

4

Clueless in the Battle

THE NATURE OF THE ARGUMENT

Arguments are a part of dating and marital life—like it or not. Couples have their own particular patterns of fighting. It may be frequent and intense, or spotty bouts of quibbling, or those once-a-year, knock-down-drag-outs. It depends on the personalities involved and their willingness to discuss or even admit their problems.

Most of the comments I've received from women deal with the problem of how to argue constructively. Most women feel that their spouses "fight dirty," avoiding the real issues and getting off on time-wasting tangents. They also say that most men are totally "clueless" in identifying the real issues involved in their fights. I've found in my research that men, for the most part, aren't clueless but rather have an unwillingness to communicate what they are really feeling. The reason for this is because men don't grow up in the same social atmosphere as women, who spend a great deal of time with each other discussing, analyzing, and identifying problems. Women are much better at this because for most of our lives, we have access to input on our problems from our girlfriends, sisters, and mothers. While men are at work, their wives are on the phone or out to lunch discussing and offering advice for each others' problems. Over the years, women develop a great deal of insight into relationship problems and how to handle them. Unfortunately, men are not afforded the same opportunity to develop this process. Unless a man has a close friend, they rarely get to air their problems with anyone else. They do not have the same kinds of support groups women have developed with each other.

Let's look at some of the most common types of arguments, and analyze what's really behind them.

#1 THE PUBLIC INSULT

The Scenario:

"I was hosting a party at my home, having a great time. I was standing with a group of people and we were discussing our pets. One woman remarked that she felt bad about having to keep her dog caged all day while she was at work. With that, my husband piped up and said 'I can relate to that! It's the story of my life—living in a cage with no freedom.'

I felt like I'd just been hit with the proverbial ton of bricks. I didn't know what to say. It was not the time or place to start a public argument so I just clammed up. Everybody was so uncomfortable. Some of my friends realized how embarrassed I was and tried to joke about it to diffuse the situation. I was so upset, I had to seek refuge in my bathroom until I calmed down.

Later on, after the guests left, I confronted him. He tried to pass it off as just a 'stupid' remark that meant nothing. I couldn't get anywhere with him, so I let it drop. But why would he do such a clueless thing?"

THE STRATEGIC ZINGER

She was angry, cut to the quick, and totally baffled. Why would he make such a cruel remark? First of all, it was no accident that he blurted out the remark in a very PUBLIC atmosphere. He COUNTED on the fact that she would not make a public scene. He not only meant to zing her, but he wanted to make his point without receiving an immediate rebuttal. Also, he gambled on the fact that by the time the guests left, she would have cooled off to a point where she might not make a "big stink" about it. Furthermore, he probably had the benefit of a couple of drinks to loosen his tongue and give him the courage it took to speak his mind.

WHAT'S THE BEST WAY TO HANDLE IT?

Let's extrapolate the scenario for the benefit of finding a solution. She was probably steaming all night, but trying to carry on with some semblance of grace. When the last guest had pulled out of the driveway, she confronted him by saying something like, "Now what the hell was that 'caged dog' remark all about?"His first response was predictable. He tried to put the onus on her by chalking it up to the fact that SHE was making a big deal out of nothing. But she needed to persist and get to the bottom of his real feelings. He obviously has been harboring a lot of anger toward her. Maybe he does feel restrained in the relationship or maybe there is another underlying cause. He wanted to hurt her with his disparaging remark, because he's very angry with her.

He chose to air it publicly because he felt safe that there could be no immediate reprisals. He is demonstrating CLASSIC "passive-aggressive" behavior. This is when you make someone pay for a perceived wrong without being the total aggressor. The "passive-aggressive" will resort to behavior that forces the other person to react. Many men do not want to get into lengthy discussions because it makes them uncomfortable. So instead, they develop this kind of "hit and run attack" method. And many women who report these kind of incidents say it's the only way their husbands know how to fight. They never hear a complaint from him when they're in private, but once they're in public, it's a different story. They never know WHAT'S going to come out of his mouth.

DROP IT OR NOT?

No, don't drop it. He has made his point. There are certain things in your relationship which bother him. Whether you think they are valid or not isn't the issue. He must learn that there is an appropriate way to vent his anger and belittling you in public is not one of them. So what you have here is a twofold problem. The first part is that he will need to learn how to communicate his feelings appropriately. The second is that you'll need to get to the root of his feelings of restriction in the relationship. He may not even be in touch with what is really bugging him. So it's going to take some hard work on both your parts to try to get to the true underlying reasons for his discontent.

COUNSELING

When anyone, male or female, has trouble identifying their problems, communicating them, and resolving them, counseling is a good idea. Otherwise, you may get into the "round and round" syndrome where you argue for hours but nothing is resolved. This is because either one or both of you are not communicating your true feelings to the other. Or in many cases, the other person is simply not ready to LISTEN. This is where an experienced person can act as an unbiased mediator and help you get directly to the heart of the matter. It will give both parties a safe environment to say what's really on their mind. A skilled counselor will help you to define and express the real issues and in many cases, work out a compromise which is agreeable to both parties.

#2 THE VERBAL ABUSER

The Scenario:

"Whenever my husband and I have a disagreement about anything, big or small, he always falls into the pattern of using foul language and name calling. This makes the argument escalate into one big, ugly arena of personal attack. I don't understand why he can't talk things over without becoming foul and abusive. When he treats me this way, I often find myself sinking to his level and returning the verbal abuse. Or sometimes, I just walk away in disgust. But when I walk away, the problem never gets solved and I build up a lot of resentment toward him. I have walled myself off emotionally from him so much that now I'm afraid our relationship can never be normal again."

THE FOUR-LETTER SYNDROME

Why does a man or a woman resort to this behavior? There can be many deep-seated psychological reasons which vary from person to person. However, one popular theory suggests that it's a learned behavior from your own parents. Both men and women tend to repeat in their own marriages what they have witnessed in their parents' relationship. And when those same people have not had the benefit of discussing the situations or really understanding their origins, they have a high probability of repeating abusive behavior. How many times have we heard that a child molester was molested himself as a child? Or a wife beater was from a home where he watched his own father beat his mother? These, unfortunately, often become the role models we carry on into our adult lives. Many men exert their "macho persona," because they have seen in their fathers how it allows them to "win" through intimidation.

Another possible explanation for this behavior is that the man is utterly lacking in the skills of communication and totally frustrated at his inability to get his feelings across. So he turns that anger toward the woman, making the disagreement a very degrading experience for her. This way, he assures his victory. He can't communicate adequately, so he turns it into a very distasteful event to make sure she won't want to communicate either. Verbal abuse is really not all that far removed from physical abuse. In the end, it accomplishes the same thing—it disheartens and wears the other person down so much that the abuser finally gets his way.

IS VERBAL ABUSE EVER JUSTIFIED?

Never. Abusers of any kind need to be made acutely aware that their behavior is totally unacceptable. It may be relatively easy to resolve early on by laying down ground rules. The FIRST foul word that is tossed at you personally will be grounds for the discussion to stop immediately until you get an apology. Sooner or later, he may "get it" and learn to stop this behavior. It is not impossible or unrealistic to try to work this out between yourselves. If he can honestly begin to see that his behavior will lead to the ultimate destruction of your relationship, he will soon change his approach.

 THE WIN-WIN APPROACH:

It is most important for women to remember that if you stoop to his level and return foul language, it will only perpetuate the problem. Granted, this is hard to do. Tempers flare and it is only natural for cuss words to fly when you're angry. But if either of you begins a tirade of foul, personal attack, you need to take a "time out." This is another instance where it would be a good idea to invoke the "penalty rule." After you have both cooled down a bit, you can resume your discussion with the promise that each cuss word will result in a "penalty." It could be monetary, or a chore performed, or whatever you agree on. This will make you both THINK before you speak and automatically cause a "time out" whenever a cuss word is used.

More often, any form of abusive behavior is deeply ingrained and therefore needs more intensive remedial action. You can benefit enormously from counseling as a couple, and he will probably need individual counseling on his own. It may take an impartial person of authority to convince him how truly destructive his behavior is to the relationship. If he grew up watching this behavior, he probably thinks that this is how ALL people handle their problems. Through counseling, he will eventually realize his behavior is dysfunctional. It may take a while before you see any positive change, but don't get discouraged. Remember, he has to deal with a lifetime of negative input.

#3 MASTER OF THE SIDE-TRACK

Many wives complained that during the course of an argument their husbands would often "get off the track." He'd throw in all kinds of extraneous issues and they both ended up arguing about everything else EXCEPT the issue at hand.

The Scenario:

"HE SAID, SHE SAID" CASE IN POINT:

SHE: *Honey, we need to do something about your mother dropping by the house unannounced. Her visits are disrupting to my schedule, time consuming, and plain inconsiderate to me. I feel like I have to sit there and entertain her, when I have many other things I should be doing.*

HE: *What, exactly, are the other things you need to do?*

SHE: *You know—things like grocery shopping, house cleaning, the usual stuff.*

HE: *Well, from the looks of this house, I've got to be honest —you don't seem to ever do much house cleaning.*

SHE: *What, exactly, is THAT remark supposed to mean?*

HE: *Now don't go getting defensive. But I am being honest. This house is always a mess. You are either out shopping or playing bridge with your girlfriends or on the phone. The house never looks neat.*

SHE: *Oh really?? Well, this is the FIRST time I've ever heard this complaint from your lips. Don't forget we have three teenagers, two dogs, and you, who all contribute to messing up the house. Do you think it's easy for me to keep up with all of you? And now, it seems you begrudge me having a little time to myself with the girls.*

ON AND ON AND ON AD NAUSEAM

...Isn't this typical? How many times has this happened to you? How many times have you said to yourself, "The man's a master at twisting everything around until I AM AT FAULT."

NO SURPRISES HERE

Think about it. What he is doing is totally AVOIDING the real issue of his mother's unannounced visits and deliberately getting you off track. Why? Because he doesn't want to address the issue at hand. He probably agrees that his mother is being intrusive and a pain-in-the-butt. But he doesn't want the responsibility of facing her with the problem and having to be the one who hurts her feelings. It's much easier to turn the issue around and make his wife go on the "defensive."

AVOIDING THE TRAP

Once you are aware of what he's doing, you can avoid the trap he usually sets up. If not, you'll be arguing about things that happened 20 years ago instead of solving the issue at hand. You'll need to stop the argument in progress by calmly saying, "We can discuss my housekeeping at another time. Right now, I am trying to enlist your help with the problem of your mother. I would appreciate it if you would confine your remarks to this ONE issue."

He may still attempt to twist the situation. But when he realizes you're not going to be sucked into the old scam, he won't have any other alternative but to address the real issue. If you are unwilling to "play his game" then the game can't continue—can it?

#4 I NEVER SAID THAT/I NEVER DID THAT

The Scenario:

"My husband suffers from a case of 'selective memory.' We get into arguments that always come down to 'his word against mine.' When I try to explain what he said to me, he denies ever saying it. He's been doing this for the fifteen years we've been married and it's so frustrating for me. He just won't take responsibility for what comes out of his mouth. Here's an example of what happens between us:

(paraphrased)

HIM: I told my boss that we would go to dinner with him on Friday night, okay?

  ME: Well, normally I'd say 'sure,' but we're having dinner with the Bensons on Friday. I asked you last week and you said it was okay with you.

HIM: You never told me the Bensons asked us for dinner. And I never would have agreed to it.

  ME: Oh yes I did. And you did agree, so I called them the next day to confirm we'd be there.

HIM: Well, you'll have to change the plans. You never asked me.

  ME: Are you losing your mind? I asked you last week at breakfast and you positively said 'yes.'

HIM: Well, I don't remember agreeing to it. Besides, you are always making plans without consulting me first.

SELECTIVE MEMORY

Granted, there are times when we all forget what we said or did. But if this is a PATTERN with your mate, it's going to be a tough one to change. The facts here aren't pretty. He is lying and he knows it. He lies because it gets him what he wants without having to face any consequences. He feels that if he doesn't admit his culpability, he can't be blamed.

We can observe this same behavior everyday in a court of law. When a witness doesn't want to admit to something because it will incriminate him, he says "I don't remember" or, "I have no recollection of saying that." With this evasive reply, he feels he can slip through the cracks. In this scenario, the husband is doing exactly the same thing with the same motivation behind it.

DEALING WITH A DENIAL

Many women believe that to be forewarned is to be forearmed. This means that you will have to be on the alert for situations you feel he will try to deny at a later time. If your husband suffers from "selective memory," it would be wise to get a large calendar and keep it in plain sight, like on the kitchen wall. If he says "yes" to that dinner date, then jot it down on the calendar in red letters while he watches you. Say "I'm marking it down on the calendar right now so WE won't forget. The "we" will allow him to feel that this action is not a punishment. Then if he develops a sudden "memory lapse" a week later when you remind him, just point to the calendar as proof positive.

When dealing with a husband who tends to develop convenient "memory lapses," you may want to try the following technique. When you have a conversation or encounter a situation which you intuitively feel he will question at a later date, speak up on the spot. Whatever he said, repeat his words back to him. Tell him you're doing this so he won't have any question about what he told you if it's brought up again. You may even go as far as jotting down his comments for future reference. Then there can be NO QUESTION later. And if you do this often enough, he may realize that his method of evasion is just not going to work anymore. It's too bad that you will be forced to resort to this tactic, but short of tape recording every conversation, there aren't many other options when dealing with this kind of personality.

The bad news is that this may not work if you are dealing with a man who lies pathologically about everything. If lying and evading are his way of life, he's going to require counseling to change his behavior. I know that it sounds discouraging when you're told that counseling is the only solution. But pathological lying is a serious character flaw that requires professional help for any lasting changes to occur. And, until he admits that what he's doing is deceitful and agrees to counseling, you're going to be saddled with a horrendous problem that won't go away.

How can you convince a person who is in total denial that he needs counseling? It isn't easy. You may have to enlist the help of other family members who are also troubled with his behavior to aid in convincing him. A clergyman or a close friend might talk to him about his problem, if you ask them for help. It isn't all that different from confronting an alcoholic with "intervention." Many times, the relationship has to be in dire straits before he will "wake up" to the fact that he's going to lose it.

#5 SILENCE IS NOT GOLDEN

The Scenario:

"My husband and I had a very heated discussion about buying a new car. I felt that we should wait for a while because our finances were not in the best shape to support such a large purchase. It would mean taking money away from more important things like the kids' education and household expenses. Not that we would starve, but it would place an extra strain on us that isn't necessary. We argued back and forth without getting anywhere. From the next day on, for over a month, he acted as cold as ice. He spoke to me only when necessary and sulked around the house making everyone's life miserable. He became irritable and short-tempered with the kids, picking on everything they did. They reacted with confusion because they didn't understand that he really wasn't angry at them. Several times, I tried to resurrect the car issue, asking if this was what was at the bottom of his silent behavior. He got very agitated and denied it, then lapsed back into his silence.

Finally after a month, I was so sick and tired of living this way, I told him to go ahead and just get the stupid car. A couple days later, he pulled into the driveway behind the wheel of a brand new BMW, grinning from ear to ear. From then on he's been pleasant and cooperative. But I'm just furious with him and even more angry at myself for giving in. What else could I do, though? Life wasn't worth living the other way.

This isn't the first time he's pulled this on me. There have been numerous occasions over the past few years when he reacted the same way. I know I made the wrong move by giving in, but I could see no other way to end the ongoing nightmare."

HOLDING HOSTAGES

Well, it appears that this husband wasn't so clueless after all. He got what he wanted by holding the whole family hostage with his silence. It's just another classic case of the good old passive-aggressive behavior working it's magic in a relationship. Kind of reminds you of the little kid who held his breath until he got what he wanted, doesn't it? Basically, this guy used the same behavioral technique. It's infantile behavior, but it's the only kind he knows that will get him results.

Think about the little kid. If he holds his breath long enough, HE WILL NOT DIE. His normal physiological processes will take over and at some point he will have to take a big gulp of air. The situation with this adult is the same. Will you dare to hold out long enough for him to take that big gulp of air? He's betting that you will give up before he does.

BACK UP YOUR OPINION WITH DATA

THE WIN-WIN APPROACH:

Don't play into his hands in a game he has created. You know WHAT he's doing and WHY he's doing it. However, you must realize that he feels he works hard for the family and is unfairly being denied something he wants. You will need to express your understanding of how HE FEELS. You might say, "Honey, I know how much you want this car. I also know how hard you work to support the family. I WANT you to have the car. It's just that right now it's not a good move financially. Let me show you what I'm basing my opinion on." Then get out a sheet of paper and show him in black and white. You may want him to finish investing in a certain CD for the kid's education. Or there may be certain credit card payments that need to be completed. But whatever, you must present a valid reason on which you've based your judgement. Then work out a compromise as to WHEN it would be advisable to purchase the car. You may find that in three months or six months or a year, after the priority obligations are taken care of, he is free to buy the car. But at least when you approach it this way, he has a definite time set in the foreseeable future when he can get what he wants. This should make him happy and much more willing to compromise.

Once you have settled the financial issue, it would be a good time to bring up your dissatisfaction with the way he has chosen to handle his problems. Ask him if a car is really worth alienating himself from the rest of the family. Tell him that in the future, you will make every effort to try to understand his point of view and arrive at a compromise. The car will be in the driveway someday, but he won't ever be able to enjoy it if it costs him the respect and love of his family to get it. It also needs to be pointed out to him that he has needlessly hurt the children. From now on, any disagreements between husband and wife should remain between them and the children must be shielded from it.

#6 TAKING THE FALL

The Scenario:

"I have been divorced for three years and recently married a divorced man who has two teenage daughters. They live with their mother. We are having a lot of problems because his kids aren't accepting me gracefully. There is always a lot of tension when they come to visit us. I feel like I am being 'tolerated' at best.

Last month, they spent the weekend with us. The 16-year-old had a date and didn't get in until 2 A.M. My husband was upset—but NOT at her. Instead, he took it out on me. He said the reason she came in so late was because I didn't stipulate a curfew time for her. He wasn't home when she left on the date, so he felt it was up to me to tell her when she was expected home. I think he's coming from left field. He has yet to say one word to her. Instead, he chooses to blame her actions on me. This is one of many instances where no matter what happens with his kids, it's always my fault."

MISDIRECTED FRUSTRATION

This situation frequently happens with divorced couples who have kids from previous marriages. The truth of the matter is that he IS angry at his daughter, but he's afraid to express his anger toward her. So guess who ends up as the scapegoat every time? And the reason he's reluctant to get into it with his daughter is because of his guilt. He feels guilty that he isn't there anymore to raise her firsthand. From her behavior, he knows his daughter is upset with him because he left the family and married another woman. So rather than taking the risk of further alienating her, he avoids having to scold her by passing blame onto his wife. It's safer to scold his wife.

This scenario is played out in a million different ways in divorced families all over the country. Any woman in a similar situation will tell you that the toughest part of marrying a divorced man is dealing with his kids. Those popular TV Sit-Coms which depict the happy-go-lucky, non-dysfunctional, perfect merging of two families are nothing but a myth. The truth is that kids from divorced families bring their own resentments, hurt feelings, and unresolved angers with them. And they have to be dealt with compassionately and with consistency. Kids of divorced parents often become very manipulative when they sense their parent's reluctance to enforce the same discipline they once did.

On the other hand, divorced parents who have part-time visitation share the very real fear of losing what little connection they have left with their kids. So you need to tread carefully here, allowing extra latitude when dealing with their fears of alienation.

PART-TIME FAMILY MANAGEMENT

In the instance where you have a part-time visitation schedule with his kids, you'll need to establish ground rules with both your husband and his kids. In the case of younger children, you should both be a part of their activities as well as their discipline. If the kids are older, as in this scenario, it would be better if you made the disciplining of his kids HIS responsibility. This is especially true when his kids are not accepting you gracefully. It will probably add to their resentment of you if the job of disciplining them is placed solely in your hands. However, in any situation where the kids are under your roof, they should have to follow rules determined by the two of you. He should not be arguing or blaming you for what his kids do. He needs to settle the problems with them by himself. You can be supportive and compassionate of his situation, but at the same time, let him know that you will no longer be the scapegoat for his kids' bad behavior. It's unfair and will undermine your relationship with him as long as it continues. When there's a recent remarriage and the kids are still a bit resentful of the new wife, she should suggest that her husband set aside some time to meet with his kids privately. He will need to discuss any problems with their behavior and enforce any punishment, himself, when appropriate. The kids should be encouraged to work on trying to improve their relationship with their step-mother. The father should encourage the kids to air their feelings about her in a non-judgmental atmosphere. After taking what they say into account, he should then ask for and offer his own suggestions which he feels might improve the situation. This will make the arena of discipline a much more comfortable situation for everyone.

These ongoing, delicate situations of trying to keep everybody happy, require an enormous amount of "give-and-take." In divorced families who share visitation rights, it has proven to be of great benefit to schedule weekly "conferences." They will provide an opportunity where everyone gets to "air" their gripes and problems. Families who do this on a regular basis usually find that these sessions are highly successful in promoting real understanding between themselves and preventing future problems. These conferences also help to foster the feeling that all the members of the new family want to accept and love one another. Everyone will learn to get along much more quickly in an atmosphere where they are not invalidating each other's feelings. It's very important that everyone in the family really LISTENS to one another's point of view so they can understand what is motivating their behavior, both positive and negative. Keeping the lines of communication open is the most effective way to accomplish the goal of maintaining harmony between all members of a broken family.

CLASSIC CLUELESS QUIP:

Men seem to forget that women have opinions that differ from their own, and it doesn't mean we don't love them. Just because we're married doesn't mean we've checked our brain at the altar.

CHAPTER $\boxed{5}$?????

The Clueless Lack of Courtesy

MISS MANNERS BE DAMNED

It's a fair statement to say that there are many men who do not practice etiquette with the same fervor as women. Why not? Did their mothers never teach them how to behave like a gentleman? Maybe not. But it's never too late to learn. There should be no excuse for a man not extending common courtesies to a woman in an adult relationship.

When men and women are dating, both are naturally on their best behavior. But as the relationship progresses, women complain that the genteel behaviors they once enjoyed from the men suddenly evaporate. We miss getting the door opened for us, polite dinner conversation, or occasional flowers. Why is it so important to us? Because it makes us feel appreciated. We naturally feel taken for granted when these things disappear from the relationship. Are they really of monumental importance? Maybe not when taken individually, but on a day-to-day basis, the lack of manners and common courtesy can erode a relationship. Kindness and courtesy are acts of appreciation and affection, and without them we feel a lot less loved. This is not to say that men are the ONLY ones who slack off in this department. Women do too. However, in the general area of what women expect from men—like pulling her chair out, opening the door, remembering her birthday, etc., most women feel that men, over time, tend to become overwhelmingly remiss.

#1 DINNER OR THE DINER?

The Scenario:

"It took me years to successfully teach my husband not to push the peas onto his dinner fork with his fingers. But what I cannot teach him is to carry on polite conversation with me during dinner. The minute dinner is served he buries his head in the plate from that moment on. He never looks up or speaks until his plate is empty. Then he looks up with a big grin on his face and wipes his mouth off on his sleeve."

WHAT ARE HER OPTIONS?

1. Hand him a bed sheet to wipe off his face after dinner.
2. Wear a teddy and fishnet stockings to dinner.
3. Flog him with the pasta until she gets his attention.

Now, I realize that these options aren't exactly what you had in mind. But after all, this specific problem can't be equated with spousal abuse. However, it is annoying and somewhat insulting to be ignored when you haven't seen each other all day.

WHAT GUYS SAY IN THEIR OWN DEFENSE

1. "I worked all day and I'm starving. I didn't figure I'd have to act like I was dining with the Queen of England."
2. "Big deal! I didn't see the napkin—so shoot me!"
3. "Would you like me to put on a tux and eat my Kraft macaroni and cheese with a silver spoon?"

TURNING THE TABLES

All kidding aside, the point here is that men do not take this table-manner thing very seriously. It all lies in your point of view. Guys see dinner as a time to feed themselves. Women see it as an opportunity to have discussions and, hopefully, feel like the dinner was appreciated by everyone. And in reality, there's no reason why there can't be some compromise.

THE WIN-WIN APPROACH:

If you find that your husband or boyfriend exhibits the same lack of manners as the man in this scenario, you should talk to him about it. Tell him that you know he's tired and just wants to enjoy his dinner in peace, but it hurts your feelings when he ignores you. Then begin a campaign to engage him in conversation at dinner. Ask him about HIS day and let him express any of his frustrations or problems without interruption. Then you can move on to other topics of interest to both of you. But save the difficult or highly emotional topics until a later time. Most men will look forward to the nightly opportunity of getting to talk about what's going on in their world. I know from experience that when a man sits down to dinner, it's the first time all day that you have him as a captive audience. And it's natural to start enumerating all the problems you've encountered with the kids, money, and a million other things. But a tired man is going to react by shutting you out. It's only natural. Be aware that nobody is at fault here. It's just the nature of married life. But you can both make a concentrated effort to turn dinner into a time of nurturing without confrontation. Once that's done, you should be able to open up the lines of communication between you.

Some men equate the practice of gentility with acting like a "sissy." It probably seems silly and excessively feminine for them to feel like they have to exhibit proper manners at all times. There are also men who simply have never been taught social graces. However, in any case, it's never too late for them to learn. If you are married or engaged to a man who truly acts like a slob at the table and constantly embarrasses you in public, then you'll need to approach this subject tactfully.

You should say something like this:

"Honey, I don't want you to take this wrong, but you need some help with your table manners. There are people who will view your lack of table manners as a sign that you just don't care enough about yourself to put some effort into how you look in public. I honestly believe you don't realize that you are presenting yourself in a bad light. So I'd like to help you correct a few of the bad habits you may not be aware of."

Then it's up to you to point out exactly what his specific problems are with his manners. He may talk with his mouth full of food, or not use his napkin correctly, or pick up food with his hands when he should be using his fork. You may even want to demonstrate how to do these things correctly. When he finally realizes how unattractive it is to talk with a mouth full of food or eat noisily, it will have a greater impact on him.

Go on to explain why good manners will make HIM a better person. "It's just a matter of putting some extra effort into eating properly. And if you don't make the effort, the truth is that people are going to categorize you as a slob.

And you deserve a lot better than that. I don't want you to continue embarrassing yourself because you're not aware of how you look to others. This is something you need to work on for yourself."

The bottom line is because you love him, you want him to be the best person he can be. And that's the truth. It's hard to argue with or become angry at the person who is lovingly trying to help you improve yourself.

#2 THE CLUELESS DRESSER

The Scenario:

"My husband and I are always fighting about the way he dresses. The man has no sense of style, color, or what looks good together. I even have to fight him to throw out his old, wide, polyester ties. If I didn't tell him what to wear, he'd go to the office looking like a bum."

MIX N' MATCH

A friend of mine made the observation: "When you're in a department store, you always see women shopping alone for their own clothes. But nine times out of ten, when a man is shopping, his wife or girlfriend accompanies him and helps pick out his wardrobe." So I went to a mall and checked it out for myself. She was right. We are all aware that most men do not like to shop with women. Likewise, there are many men who hate or refuse to shop for themselves. Women are always saying that their men haven't got a clue as to what "goes together" when trying to assemble a wardrobe. My Mom always teases my Dad by reminding him that if she didn't check out what he put on, he'd leave the house wearing a red plaid sports coat with green striped pants. Other women say they have to label their husband's clothes in color-coded fashion, like they did when they bought Garanimals for their kids. The fact is that men as a rule are simply not as fashion conscious as women are. They just don't feel that fashion should be such a "big deal." They probably think it's just plain stupid to be so obsessed with what they're wearing and just don't want to spend the extra time it takes to co-ordinate an outfit. And while most men view clothes as just something to wear, women believe that clothes make a definite statement about "who you are."

NO BIG CRIME COMMITTED HERE

Okay, so it's not really a big deal. But I think it's important for men to realize that in the business world or in social situations, people do tend to judge you by your appearance. And, if you look like "Bozo the Clown" in a mismatched outfit, you're going to be looked upon as having a "Bozo" mentality. Sure, it's unfair and shallow. But it's a fact that society judges the success of a person by how he dresses.

THE WIN-WIN APPROACH:

So, if your mate hates to shop, do it for him. It's important for his image to arrive at work looking neat, well-groomed and dressed nicely. It's not placing too big a burden on a wife to make sure that her husband looks presentable. It's just a part of loving and looking after him. You do it for your kids, so you can do it for your spouse too. But you'll need to approach the subject with diplomacy because you don't want him to feel like he's such a moron you have to dress him. You might start out by saying the following:

"You know Honey, it's been a long time since you bought any new clothes for yourself. I know you hate to shop, so how about if I do it for you. I'd like to get you a few new outfits. Your shirts are fraying around the collars and you could use a new sports jacket or two with some matching pants. I'm going shopping at a store that's got some great bargains, so maybe I'll pick up a couple of things for you while I'm at it."

Then go out and stock up on color-coordinated sports jackets and slacks, shirts and classy ties. And on weekends, if he wants to loll around the house in sweats and a ripped up shirt, let him. As long as you've got him covered properly during the week, I would cut him a break on the weekends. It's not too big a compromise in the scheme of things.

#3 THE HYGIENICALLY CHALLENGED

The Scenario:

I received a number of letters from women who complained about their hygienically clueless husbands. They say that the cute, sweet-smelling, well-bred guy they married has, over the years, mutated into a major dirt bag. Here are some of their comments; followed by my suggestion of some behavior therapy...

1. *"He never wears deodorant anymore. He smells like a sweaty ol' locker room."*

   HOW TO COPE: Leave a giant-sized can of deodorant on his side of the bed. Attach a note saying, "Do your part to clean up the environment."

2. *"He has the disgusting habit of going to the toilet and missing, so I'm stuck cleaning up the dribble stains all around the base of the bowl."*

   HOW TO COPE: Paint a bulls-eye inside the toilet bowl.

3. *"As he gets older, it seems he's getting more and more flatulent. It's so gross—he breaks wind in public all the time. And it doesn't even embarrass him."*

   HOW TO COPE: Give him a personalized cork.

4. *"My husband leaves his dirty underpants, socks, shirts, etc. strewn all over the room. No matter how much I nag and bitch, I can't get him to pick up after himself. Didn't his mother ever teach him anything?"*

   HOW TO COPE: Install a basketball hoop above the hamper.

5. *"He comes to bed without brushing his teeth, shaving, or taking a shower. Then he has the nerve to complain that I never want sex anymore. Can you blame me?"*

   HOW TO COPE: Put a note on his pillow—"No shower, no shave— NO SEX."

WHEN IT'S NO JOKE

Although it's fun to joke about it, a man's poor personal hygiene habits can be a big turnoff for his wife. Granted, it's not the end of the world or a cause to run to a divorce lawyer. But it IS offensive. Many women take it as a personal slight. They feel that if he doesn't care enough to clean himself for them, then he must not care much about them. There are some women who are willing to overlook bad hygiene and some who aren't. It's a matter of the extent to which it offends them. Here's how the majority of women feel about these subjects:

In The Matter Of Personal Cleanliness:

Most women take the position that if the man is remiss, he needs to take remedial action. Most women make the effort to be as desirable as possible when making love with him. They shower, apply perfume, and shave their legs. So she has every right to complain when he comes to bed with bad breath and body odor. But when you send him back to the bathroom to clean up, promise him it will be worth his efforts. Then deliver on that promise. It won't take long until he associates a clean body with great sex.

In The Matter Of Neatness:

Some men will never agree to pick up after themselves. Sometimes it seems like it's just not programmed into the genes of the male species. Besides, they think anything connected to "laundry" is a woman's job. Many women just accept it because they feel that the nagging they'd have to do to get him to pick up after himself just isn't worth the effort. However, if you are a working spouse, you'll probably feel that he has an obligation to split many of the household chores with you. You both have got to set aside some time to make up a list of designated responsibilities. It should be based on the number of hours you work, what time you get home from work, and the ability to perform them successfully. For example, you may cook dinner every night but he has to clean up and stack the dishwasher. You might do the laundry, but he is responsible for putting his clothes back into the drawers and closet.

Obviously, there's going to be a lot of compromise in this situation depending upon things which arise during the week. However, if he begins to shirk a lot of his chores, DO NOT do them for him. Even if his clean clothes you laundered pile up to the ceiling and he still doesn't put them away—leave them there. A woman is just as tired as a man when she gets home after putting in an eight-hour work day. And it's important that the man be held accountable for his share of household work.

In The Matter Of Excessive Flatulence:

The cause is most likely his diet. Try getting him to change some of the foods he eats and see if this doesn't help. Milk products and certain legumes are notorious for causing gas. If this doesn't help, then ask him to please go to another room whenever he feels the urge. Tell him that you find it offensive and discourteous. However, most women agree that guys think farting is funny. It usually doesn't embarrass them at all. So this may be one of those problems you will unfortunately be stuck with for as long as he's around.

#4 THE GARBAGE MOUTH

The Scenario:

"My husband has a mouth like a garbage can. It's bad enough that I'm subjected to it in private, but when we go out in public, he's always telling filthy jokes in mixed company. I've asked him, for my sake, to please clean up his language. I guess he's either unwilling or unable to stop because he's still doing it. I'm fed up with arguing with him about it."

MALE MENTALITY

Many men are totally clueless when it comes to understanding that foul language is offensive to most women. Swearing seems to be the only means they have to express themselves. They have no idea how harshly these words impact on others. These men have grown up believing that being foul-mouthed makes them appear cool. They operate from a distorted sense of values where foul-mouthed equals macho equals admiration. And, if the joke gets a big laugh, it acts as an additional ego-stroker for him. Also, some men get a sense of power from the shock value their foul language evokes.

I think we would all agree that the woman who wrote this criticism has a valid complaint. If you share a problem similar to her's, there are some things you'll need to be aware of when taking steps to correct the situation. If you insist that your husband stops telling dirty jokes in public, then you must never laugh when another man does it. He'll make sure to hurl this back at you and it will give him the validation he needs to continue his behavior.

As with any type of ongoing negative situation, the person has to be educated as to why his behavior is inappropriate. The strength of your argument must lie in the fact that foul language reflects very badly upon him as a person. You'll need to explain to him that women often disguise their disapproval when offended by his remarks. This is only because they don't want to make a scene or embarrass themselves by chastising the offending party in public. But the majority of women, including yourself, are not only disgusted by the language, but also by the PERSON who is USING the language. The message he's giving is that he doesn't have enough respect for the women he's addressing to clean up his mouth. It becomes especially insulting if he does it amongst a group of strangers. When he's with long-standing friends whom he knows aren't offended by the dirty jokes or bad language, he can get away with it. But it is highly inappropriate to do it in any other situation. And if the company is a mixture of friends and strangers, it is still a bad idea. There is no way of knowing beforehand how any stranger will react to crude language.

If you are ALWAYS offended by dirty talk, then it's your right to walk into another room and not be subjected to it. Most offenders seldom stop to think that talking this way demeans them as a person. But only if they truly UNDERSTAND that it does, will they be willing to make an attempt to change.

#5 THE SEXUAL BRAGGART

The Scenario:

"My husband and I have been married for five years. Before that, we had both been single for a number of years and each had several long-term relationships. Our marriage is happy except for one problem which is driving me crazy. Whenever we are out with friends, he seizes every opportunity to interject details about one of his past sexual relationships with some "hot babe." Not only that, but he often relates embarrassing details of some of OUR sexual exploits! It hurts and humiliates me. I've told him how I feel, but he keeps doing it. The man doesn't have a clue as to how tacky his behavior is, how bad it makes me look, and how insulted it makes me feel."

THE NEED TO LOOK MACHO

Well, guess what? It's a case of the old "High School Harry" behavior rearing its ugly head. And it sounds like he behaves this way because he still measures his worth by his sexual prowess. He must feel terribly inadequate somewhere deep-down in his repeated attempt to gain "admiration" for his acts. Remember back in high school when a guy had sex with a girl and then spread it all over school the next day? In effect, he's doing the same thing. When he brags about his sexual conquests, it reassures him that he is still sexy and cool.

RE-EDUCATING HIM

Men who resort to this kind of behavior need to be re-educated in the world of ADULT values. And you're the one who has to do it. You'll need to explain that no one is going to think BETTER of him after he gets through bragging. On the contrary, they will think WORSE of him. Have him put the shoe on the other foot for a moment. Ask him how he would feel if you publicly talked about some hot sexual encounters you shared with a few old boyfriends. Wouldn't he feel hurt and betrayed? Wouldn't it make you look cheap and promiscuous? If he's being honest, he will agree it does. Let him know that his stories about the past also make you look like you're failing him in some way in the present. It's like saying you are not living up to the fun that he had before he met you.

It's predictable that he will maintain that it's DIFFERENT for a man. He will probably say that people aren't shocked, they actually enjoy hearing it. But this simply isn't true. Decent people keep their bedroom antics between themselves. The details of their private sexual interaction should NEVER be for anyone else's ears. What woman wants the details of her orgasms or sexual behavior related in lurid detail in public? What's the point of publicly humiliating her?. I would even go one step further and warn him that his discussions of your sexual habits are actually INHIBITING your sex life with him. And if he doesn't keep his mouth shut, it's going to make your sex life deteriorate to a point where you're both miserable.

If he's at all reasonable, he will stop this behavior. However, I'm willing to bet that there are an awful lot of men who wouldn't change until their sex lives actually begin to suffer. The threat may just not be enough. I would handle it this way. The next time he tells a private sexual thing about you in public, you should refuse to have sex with him the next time he wants it. I would say "You know, I've told you again and again that what you're doing is positively HUMILIATING to me. After the way you've made me feel, the last thing I want to do is make love to you. I don't feel like making love to someone who has degraded me." There has to be a CONSEQUENCE for his actions in order for him to stop behaving this way. If you stick to this position every time he does it, he's going to get the message loud and clear.

THE WIN-WIN APPROACH:

But don't forget to reward him on the occasions when he remains closed mouthed in public. You can say, "Honey, I know you had an opportunity at the party tonight to brag about our sex life—but you didn't. I want to thank you for respecting my feelings. I love you for that." Then reward him with a big kiss or something better...you should be in the mood for it this time!

If your man doesn't respond to this method, then apparently his need to bolster his own ego borders on "dysfunctional." Unfortunately, in this case, he is going to require professional counseling if any change is to be effected.

#6 WILL SOMEBODY PLEASE OPEN THE DOOR?

The Scenario:

"My boyfriend and I have been going together for about three years. We have a good, compatible relationship. I don't know if it's going to end in marriage because we both have been divorced, are in our 40's, and see no rush.

The area in which my boyfriend is totally clueless is our constant battle about his refusal to open the car door for me. It may sound like a trivial thing, but it's one about which I have firm convictions. I feel that it is important that he extend me this small courtesy. When he leaves me to get out of the car by myself, it makes me feel like I'm not important enough for him to bother. And frankly, I like the idea of a man opening the door for me. I have told him a thousand times that I really want him to do this for me, but he won't budge. When I ask him why he won't do this for me, he says, 'it's stupid and unnecessary.' He tells me I am 'perfectly capable of opening the door for myself.'

If he would only extend this small courtesy to me, he'd find that I'd reciprocate the kindness back to him in a million different ways. Subconsciously, it's probably one of the reasons I'm having trouble committing to him for life. His obvious lack of regard for my feelings gnaws away at me. I keep wondering, what's next? I don't know why he just can't wise up and see that it will benefit him too."

THE DOOR TO DISCOVERY

Surprisingly, this is a common issue between men and women. Probably well over half of all men don't open doors for their wives or girlfriends. It all boils down to this: she has asked for a small courtesy to be extended to her. Realistically, it is no "skin off his nose" to open the car door for her. But he vehemently refuses to do this for her. Why? Who knows? It could take a battery of psychiatrists fifty years to uncover his true motivations. Maybe his mother slammed the car door on his finger when he was two years old. But the truth is that it doesn't matter what the cause is. What matters is that he is being selfish and uncompromising about performing a small act of kindness toward her. His intractability is something she needs to examine carefully to see if it also pervades into his attitude, in general, towards her.

SHOULD SHE SHUT THE DOOR FOR GOOD?

How far do you think she should push this issue? There is no simple answer. She has to weigh this one ongoing problem against his over-all attitude towards her in their relationship. If the car door issue is an isolated one and he's cooperative in everything else, then she shouldn't use it as a reason to end the relationship. However, there are a lot of relationships in which the "car door" may be just one of many areas where a man shows lack of consideration for his partner. If you are involved with a man who behaves stubbornly and inconsiderately in many areas of your relationship and it is seriously troubling you, then you'll need to evaluate the reasons why you're remaining with him.

THE WIN-WIN APPROACH:
Women who share a similar problem might consider the "trade-off" approach—for example, "if YOU open the car door for me, then I'LL change one of my behaviors that annoys you." I don't think that this is an unfair concession for a woman to make. After all, women have their inconsiderate moments, too. The "trade-off" approach will also heighten your awareness about the areas in which each of you can make improvements. It's a winning solution for both parties.

After reading the various scenarios in this book, I think you'll agree that it's a difficult prospect to CHANGE anyone else's behavior. Marriage is a series of compromises, even between couples who get along fairly well. But if you start out with a relationship where the man shows little or no consideration for you in most areas, the odds of attaining real harmony are just about impossible.

CLASSIC CLUELESS QUIPS:

#1 [Father getting the daughter dressed:]
"Do the panties go OVER or UNDER the tights?

#2 "My husband makes me feel like the Queen of England—he always walks five feet behind me."

CHAPTER 6

No Thanks from the Clueless Man

THE THANKLESS JOBS

It's not unusual for a woman to suffer a great deal of aggravation because she feels she's constantly being taken for granted. You've heard the old adage: "A woman's work is never done." This is so true because women have to wear so many different "hats" in their daily lives. Among them:

WIFE/SIGNIFICANT OTHER	LOVER
MOTHER	NURSE
CHAUFFEUR	HOUSE CLEANER/MAID
REFEREE	EMPLOYEE/VOLUNTEER
COUNSELOR	TEACHER
COOK	LOVING DAUGHTER
SOCIAL DIRECTOR	FASHION CONSULTANT
CPA	LAUNDRESS/IRONER

....and many more as we go through various stages of our lives.

Like any responsible person, we feel a need to do these jobs well. We put a lot of pressure on ourselves to keep our husbands, kids, and everyone else we love cared for and happy. And for much of the time it's a thankless job. Even though they may appreciate all you do for them, they seldom take the time to thank you. Husbands can be especially clueless when it comes to showing appreciation. Over the course of a marriage they come to "expect" things to be done for them. But if they just took two seconds to say "thank you" for our efforts they would get even more from us. Sometimes women just "give up" because they aren't receiving those necessary 'strokes' for their efforts.

#1 THANKS A LOT!

The Scenario:

"My husband came home and asked me to put together a sit-down dinner to benefit his favorite charity in two weeks. I busted my buns to get it together—flowers, bartender, rental tables, and the caterer. That evening our living room had been cleared of all the furniture. It looked wonderful— eight tables decorated like the White House. The children were shipped off to stay with good friends. All my husband had to do was show up looking great.

The evening turned out to be a smashing success. My husband was thrilled at the amount of the contributions. After the last guest left, I picked up the children only to find my youngest daughter with a massive headache. While tucking her into bed I called down to my husband to bring up some aspirin and a glass of water. He replied, "Can't you see how exhausted I am? Don't bother me with the children. PLEASE!"

WHO DID WHAT FOR WHOM?

I'll bet most women in this situation would have felt like killing this guy. Didn't he have a clue as to the amount of effort, planning, and running around his wife did to pull off this event? After his inconsiderate remark, I'm sure she wished she had served hot dogs and beans on paper plates.

This is a typical case of a man "shooting himself in the foot." For many women, that party would have been the LAST party she'd ever throw for his benefit. How dumb of him. It would have taken so little to make her happy. He should have picked up the kids, put them to bed, and then told her for the rest of the evening what a marvelous job she had done. Then they would have both been happy and able to share in the glow of a successful evening together. Instead, he hurt her feelings and made her feel taken for granted. So each went to bed in stony silence. His behavior was not only selfish but self-defeating too. Showing appreciation for someone else's efforts is a basic ingredient in a successful relationship.

SHOULD SHE JUST FORGET IT?

It all depends on how far she wants to push the issue. She could have explod-ed and had a major battle on her hands. Or she can suffer for weeks in silent resentment. However, it's important for all women to remember that some-one can take advantage of you ONLY IF YOU LET THEM. If you are a woman who is faced with a similar situation, you should sit down with your husband and tell him that you feel his behavior is extremely selfish. You should say, "You know something, Honey? If it had been anybody else other than me putting in all the effort, you would have thanked them for months. And if you don't wake up to your own insensitivity, the next time you can just hire a full staff to stage the entire event."

Sometimes we women do our jobs TOO WELL. By that, I mean that often a woman can make a huge undertaking seem effortless. But in reality, it takes a ton of extra effort to make it look "effortless." This is what men don't real-ize. Just because we're not running around like a wild-woman the night of the party doesn't mean it was EASY. To save money there's a lot of leg work we do ourselves instead of hiring someone else to do it. It is a woman's pleasure to support her husband. However, no woman needs to be a martyr. When a man is continually unappreciative of your efforts, then he needs to have it pointed out to him. If he admits that he was acting callously and assures you that he won't do it again, then you should give it another try. If the same thing hap-pens a second time, then you should tell him that you will no longer volun-teer to stage an event for him. Hopefully, when he has to shell out the money and take the time to do a lot of the planning himself, he'll realize how much effort you put into doing it for him. Unfortunately, there are many people who never learn anything unless they learn it "the hard way."

#2 WHAT A GAS

The Scenario:

"Every time I borrow my husband's car, the gas tank is on empty. I com-plain constantly, telling him that it's indicative of the bigger problems he has of shirking common everyday details and responsibilities. He really can't come up with much to justify his behavior so he tosses out this truly inane explanation:

"It's better not to drive with a full tank in the event of an accident. The impact could cause a huge gasoline explosion."

IT RANKS UP THERE...

Well gals, you've got to admit that this one ranks up there with the best of them. We must give him this much—he's certainly creative!

THE WIN-WIN APPROACH:

The gas issue is a symptom of the larger problem of shirking responsibility in everyday matters. There are a lot of women who complain that their husbands go to work, come home, and feel their job ends here. But in reality, there are hundreds of big and small chores at home which need the man's attention. Instead of sitting around doing a 'slow burn' women have to learn to speak up. Sit down with your partner and work out a schedule of designated responsibilities. He might agree to keep the checkbook in order, get the car washed, and keep the garage clean. You might prefer to do the gardening, take the trash out, and drop off clothes at the cleaners. Then there should be individual responsibilities like keeping your own clothes picked up off the floor or cleaning the shower stall after each one uses it.

Maybe it would be interesting to "reverse" chores once in a while. For example, the woman could wash the car and the man does the laundry. It's a great learning experience and it keeps the chores from becoming too monotonous. But it doesn't matter who does what, only that you reach agreement and both live up to your end of the bargain. Naturally, nothing is perfect. There will be plenty of times when one of you forgets. When this happens, be gracious and do it for each other. But at least when you have a division-of-labor plan working for you, you'll be a lot more willing to compromise when it becomes necessary.

#3 THE BIRTHDAY/ANNIVERSARY BLACK HOLE

The Scenario:

"Every time it's my birthday my husband does either of these two things:
a. He forgets the date completely and gets no card, much less a gift.
b. Tells me he has "ordered" something for me and I'll get it "next week."

On one particular birthday, he arrived home from work late (he had stopped and had a 'few for the road') with an unsigned card, a generic cake, and cellophane-wrapped flowers in a supermarket bag. I was so disgusted by his transparent attempt at thoughtfulness, I took the bag and dumped it, contents and all, into the trash compactor. He was utterly flabbergasted!!"

HEROINE OR VILLAINESS?

Some of you will be thinking, "Right on! The babe has guts! That's what I've always felt like doing but never had the nerve to actually go through with it." Others will feel that at least he did SOMETHING and he deserved better treatment.

The key is in how much importance you attach to these occasions. However, I think the majority of women are hurt and disappointed when they receive no gift or one with no more than five seconds of thought behind it. And if you feel this way you don't have to be a door mat. Just tell him how rotten he is making you feel with his obvious lack of forethought.

WHY MEN ARE CLUELESS

Most men simply don't possess the same kind of sentimentality about these occasions as women do. To them, it's just one more thing they feel pressured to remember. Women, on the other hand, see it as a time to get some special attention. And if he doesn't care enough to remember you properly once or twice a year, he's a jerk. But how do you make him come to share the importance with you? Lecturing usually gets you nowhere. Why? Because there needs to be something in it FOR HIM, too. Here's a great method one woman shared with me.

THE WIN-WIN APPROACH:

On every anniversary she rents a wonderfully romantic hotel room for the weekend. She lets him know ahead of time that this is going be one HOT weekend. The one sure-fire way to GET HIS ATTENTION every time is to allude to sex. She suggests he buy her a sexy nightie and she gets him something equally as stimulating like silk boxers—and voila! After enjoying great sex, a bottle of champagne, and lots of nurturing romance together, their anniversary is the one date he always marks on the calendar in big red letters.

This is an example of creative compromising that will get you everywhere. It can work for birthdays or other occasions too. If you can't afford the hotel, then farm the kids out for a night and do it at home. Candles, wine, and a cozy dinner followed by a romantic romp in your bedroom will have the same effect.

#4 THE SELF-SUFFICIENT WOMAN

This story is from a very happily married woman of twelve years. Her husband is in television production and spends a great deal of time away from home in a very time-consuming business. She has learned to be extremely independent because she has to cope with her children, family problems, and managing much of the day-to-day agenda on her own. She is totally understanding and accepting of that fact and for the most part he is very appreciative of her. But in one area she had a big problem.

The Scenario:

"Whenever my husband and I had a social engagement to attend I usually drove there by myself. Because of his busy schedule, he would leave from the studio and meet me wherever the party was being held. This part was okay with me. But at the end of the evening, he would head for his car, leaving me to walk back to my car alone. Sometimes I had to walk through a dark parking lot or down a poorly lighted street to get to my car. It has really bothered me for years, but I felt it wasn't worth making an issue over. I know that he sees me as being so independent and strong that he never gave it a second thought. He thinks there's nothing I can't do alone because I've always managed so well.

One night as we were leaving the studio I walked alone to my car, as usual. A friend remarked to my husband, 'Are you nuts? Why do you let her walk to her car alone?'

He replied, 'Well, she ALWAYS does that. She doesn't mind. She's very capable of taking care of herself.'

When we got home, he told me about the conversation. And when I finally told him that it DID bother me very much, he was absolutely SHOCKED."

A JOB DONE TOO WELL

This is a case where the woman has learned to manage her life SO well that her husband was entirely clueless to the fact that she could be vulnerable in any situation. At first, he was angry that an issue had been made about her going alone to her car. He felt that because she had never said anything about it, she was perfectly agreeable with the situation. But after a lengthy discussion, he began to realize that there were a lot of instances in which he left her totally vulnerable. After that night, she has never gone unescorted to her car again.

IF YOU DON'T ASK FOR HELP, YOU AIN'T 'GONNA GET IT

Her husband was clueless, because SHE didn't clue him in. It's hard to blame someone for a situation you allow to go unmentioned for years. So ladies, if you find yourself in any situation that you're uncomfortable with, it's your duty to inform him. It's not nagging or bitching. Your safety or well-being HAS to take a priority here. And if YOU don't make it a priority, he certainly never will. This is not a case of blame either. It's just a matter of informing him that your needs aren't being met and asking him to do something about it.

#5 IN SICKNESS AND IN HEALTH

The Scenario:

This story is so cute and so typical of the clueless man I had to share it so we could all enjoy a good chuckle.

"I thought my hubby was pretty sharp, but last week I had the flu and asked him to bring home dinner. I had in mind something warm and cozy...but he comes home with lettuce, bean sprouts, pea pods and mushrooms. I had nausea to begin with and the sight of those raw veggies made me even queasier.

Of course, he did a little pouting because I didn't want to eat the "dinner" he brought home for his sick wife! He said he had a bad day and couldn't think of what to bring me. He ate a salad and I made a TV dinner for myself. He didn't have a clue how to take care of his wife when she had the flu."

TILL DEATH (FROM DINNER) DO US PART

I can just hear my female readers cracking up over this story. Boy, is he ever typical of a "clueless" man or what? You know that women are not supposed to get sick, ever! And if and when they dare to, men fall apart. Did you ever try sending your man to the grocery store with a list and he returns with everything on the shelves EXCEPT what was on the list?

The answer to this problem is that there is no real answer. When a wife gets sick, men are notorious for being the worst nurses on Earth. When you're out of commission it totally upsets their universe. They panic if they have to make dinner. They hate to eat alone and don't know what to do with the dishes. But most of all, even if they won't admit it, they're frightened because you're sick. They just want you to hurry up and get better. So do the best you can and appreciate the fact that he loves you so much.

But whatever you do—don't ask him to do the laundry unless you want to be wearing all pink clothes!!

CLASSIC CLUELESS QUIPS:

#1 **"Honey, I can't find my _____ "** (fill in the blank).
[over a millions items to choose from]

Wives are expected to be psychics and locate everything from lost keys to tax returns from 1978.

#2 You have had a headache for three days and ask him in a moment of panic if he thinks it could be a brain tumor. He answers, "It couldn't be very large if you do."

7

Cheaters Who Leave Clues

SOME MEN WILL BE BOYS

Most women accept the fact that men will be men. What does this mean? For most of us, it means that men will always LOOK when a pretty woman walks by, enjoy viewing a centerfold (they'll admit only to the interview section), and fantasize about having great sex with other women. We accept this. But men will be BOYS when they carry it too far and make their partners feel insecure and uncomfortable. Women will always take a dim view of excessive ogling, flirting, and voyeurism. These behaviors represent red flags when practiced to extremes by their husbands or men with whom they share a committed relationship.

How much of this behavior should a woman tolerate in a relationship? I think that when a man is severely testing your limits of tolerance on a continuing basis some changes have to be made. First, we need to evaluate our relationship and honestly admit if there are problems which are making him behave this way. There are some hard questions which need to be answered. Is your sex life unsatisfactory for both of you or is he constantly complaining he isn't getting enough sex? Is this true? Why? If not, was he always a man who had a roving eye? If so, did you expect him to change once he was married?

But there is a bottom line which should be drawn by all women. *Looking is one thing, but cheating is another.* No woman should tolerate cheating in a marriage. Both parties take a sacred oath of fidelity in marriage. And once that's violated a woman needs to take serious measures to either dissolve the marriage or seek counseling to try and rebuild the relationship. Many find it impossible to ever reestablish trust in the man again. If she never truly forgives him and remains suspicious of his every move then the marriage is merely a shell. Forgiving one who has betrayed you is certainly not impossible, but it will take an enormous amount of work for both parties. Their lines of communication are going to have to become incredibly strong to keep connected. I personally feel that if there is ever a need for counseling, this is it. Because it's such an emotional issue, I think that an objective third party can help you clarify what happened, why it happened, and how to constructively work through it. You are going to have to learn how to deal with your anger, mistrust, and battered self-esteem. I feel that counseling will give you the best possible chance to do that.

But a woman has to be realistic about her situation. If the man isn't willing to change and continues to cheat—then for all practical purposes, *there is NO marriage.*

#1 THE PERPETUAL FLIRT

The Scenario:

"I have been married for four years to a man I dated in college. He is a good husband for the most part and treats me very well. But when it comes to going out with other couples or going to parties, his behavior is insulting. He blatantly flirts with every woman in the room. Five minutes after we arrive, he's off chatting and falling all over himself in front of some pretty girl. The last time we were at a party, he spent 45 minutes making an ass of himself over some bimbo in a low cut dress with her boobs hanging out. I was furious and had to practically drag him away from her.

When we got home we had a giant fight. He maintains that he's doing 'nothing wrong'—merely talking and socializing. He accuses me of being oversensitive and jealous. He can't understand why I would get so upset because after all, he 'ISN'T CHEATING' on me. I told him how miserable his flirting makes me feel, but he insists I'm being 'unreasonable.' He makes me upset and miserable and then he acts like I don't have a right to feel this way."

GUESS WHAT? HE'S NOT SO CLUELESS

First of all, why is this woman claiming that he is a "good husband for the most part?" He is making her miserable. Besides, he has EVERY clue how he's making her feel because she has told him so. His way of dealing with it is to invalidate her feelings so he can continue on with his behavior. This demonstrates his obsessive need to flirt because it fulfills some deep void in him. He rationalizes that as long as he's not SLEEPING with another woman any other behavior is "harmless." But this is far from the truth. His behavior is not only childish, it is degrading to her.

CHOICES

Many women who are treated this way feel demeaned and powerless to change it. But in reality, they are not powerless. They do have choices. Here are some actions other women have taken to deal with this problem:

1. Stick like glue to his side at parties. If she sees him getting too chummy with a woman she'll steer him in another direction.
2. Demand that they both leave the party the minute he starts flirting.
3. Refuse to go out socially with him anymore until he stops the behavior.
4. Insist that they both go to counseling to get at the root of his need to flirt with other women.

I would advise any woman who shares a similar problem to discuss these choices with your husband. You should make it clear that you are no longer going to tolerate any form of his flirting. And what's more, his justification that what he's doing is "harmless" just won't cut it. In truth, it's degrading and you need to tell him that it is destroying your feelings for him. Remind him that you are both in this marriage and if he is seriously having problems being WITH YOU, then he better be honest about it. He's going to need to get his true feelings "out in the open" before you can deal with them. Then you're going to have to do a lot of listening to each other before you can begin to repair the problems.

Some men will tell you that they honestly don't know why they feel compelled to flirt. They will stick to the premise that it's "just a guy thing" and continue to do it despite your protests. However, once you have decided that you can no longer live with this behavior, let him know you MEAN BUSINESS. Stick to your convictions and don't let him talk you into accepting any behavior less than what you expect. You can count on the fact that he's going to try. In any event, I think counseling is definitely needed if the flirting continues. Often, a woman remains in denial about serious problems going on between her and her husband. Flirting with every woman at a party is not "normal" married behavior. It is the behavior of a man who is still "looking."

And even though it's the guy who owns the problem, the woman who marries him is going to inherit it. Realistically, any woman who goes ahead and marries a man who constantly flaunts flirtatious behavior in her face is a woman who is courting disaster.

#2 WHEN THE CLUELESS ONE LEAVES CLUES

This woman writes of her saga after the fact. She says that after six years of marriage, she suspected her husband of having an affair with a co-worker:

The Scenario:

"He wasn't even smart about it. I found motel, restaurant, and even jewelry receipts stashed away in his sock-drawer. The phone would ring at odd hours and when I answered it the other party would hang up. There were also countless 'business' dinners, 'errands' at odd hours, and other excuses he'd invent to leave the house.

After several months of denial, he finally admitted it. We tried counseling, but it proved ineffective. The hurt and betrayal were just too massive to overcome. I felt he was only going to counseling to make himself look less like 'the bad guy' in my eyes. He was obviously in love with the other woman. We eventually got divorced. But it was a bitter, degrading ordeal because he was so dishonest with me throughout the whole affair. I was so angry with him that the entire divorce became my personal quest to get even with him. But I eventually got over it and I'm happily re-married. But I will never forget what a clueless jerk he turned out to be."

STATING THE OBVIOUS

I doubt there is a woman out there who hasn't heard a story like this one. No matter what the circumstances were leading up to the betrayal and subsequent divorce, one thing is crystal clear. He left clues because HE WANTED TO GET CAUGHT.

Let's face it. Affairs are hard to hide, but many people do it successfully for years by being extremely careful. But when a man is so careless as to leave evidence around and makes only a half-hearted attempt to cover his tracks, he wants to get caught. Why? Because he wants out of the marriage. In this case, he didn't have the guts to "come clean" and ask for a divorce. He did it the cowardly way by leaving enough clues to get caught. By doing it this way, he avoided his responsibility of facing her with the truth like a man. Or maybe he was playing for more time to insure the affair was going to last.

The fact remains that he really wasn't clueless at all. It was part of his plan all along. By the time he was leaving clues obvious enough for a potted fern to figure out, you can bet he was already committed to the other woman. He was ready to be "found out" and get on with his new life. But he wasn't ready to be a man and tell his wife the truth.

CONFRONTING THE PROBLEM

If you are trying to cope with the dilemma of a cheating husband the first thing you must do is face the problem head on. Confront him. The worst thing you can do is remain in denial and ignore the clues, hoping it will eventually go away. Even if it does, you're going to lose your self-respect and self-esteem in the process. You're never going to be able to trust him again if you don't find out what things were lacking in your marriage that motivated him to have an affair. You can't correct a problem if you don't know what's causing it.

Once it's all out in the open you've got some hard questions to ask him. Is he in love with the other woman? Is he planning to leave the marriage? If he is, then for your own sanity, you've got to let him go. And then you've got a lot of work to do to move on with your own life and put all your efforts into making it a happy and productive one. One of the saddest things to see is a woman who gets "stuck in a pattern of revenge" against an ex-husband. While he has moved on into a happy relationship, she wastes the best years of her life trying to "get back at him." It's totally counter-productive to her finding her own happiness.

It doesn't matter if your husband was the biggest bastard on Earth. You have got to think about yourself now. Your energies need to be spent building back your self-confidence and self-worth. Obviously it's not going to happen immediately and it's not going to be easy. But we can all "grow" from bad experiences if we put the knowledge to use constructively. If you feel that you're going to require help to do it don't be afraid to ask for it. There are support groups, counseling services, and the love of your family to guide you every step of the way. Take advantage of the help available, do not try to do it alone!

#3 WHO HAD THE CLUE?

The Scenario:

"For years my husband was the biggest flirt on earth. No matter where we'd go together, he'd take every opportunity to cozy up to some bimbo and leave me standing there alone. He'd ogle every teeny-bopper in the mall making comments like 'boy is this one hot-to-trot', or that one was 'ripe

for the picking,' or how he could 'get lost in those jugs,' on and on ad nauseam.

We had hundreds of major battles about his flirting. I would tell him over and over how worthless he made me feel. He'd stick to the principle that he wasn't 'screwing' them, but 'just looking.' So what was the big deal? The sad truth was that my feelings never mattered to him. I had threatened for years that the next time he fell all over a woman I'd leave him. I must have made that threat more than a thousand times. And guess what? One day I did it. I had simply reached my saturation point. We were at a party and he was drunk and slobbering all over some bleached blond. He kept it up for the entire evening. Well, something in me just snapped that night. I was hurt and humiliated for the last time. The next morning I told him to get out. It was over.

His reaction was TOTAL DISBELIEF. He didn't have a clue as to how I could be so 'unforgiving and hard-hearted.' I felt his reaction was almost laughable after all the pain and suffering I endured because of him. After warning him thousands of times I would leave him if he did it ONE MORE TIME, he had the nerve to act shocked. It's laughable. How one man could be so blind is beyond belief."

HE GOT THE CLUE

This man didn't have A clue, he had THOUSANDS of them. But the one thing he counted on was that she'd never go through with her threats. She cried wolf so many times, he went through years of complacently feeling that she'd never make a move. So when she did he was completely shocked. But it must be pointed out that she was co-dependent in a relationship which enabled him to continue his behavior. For years she made idle threats, but unfortunately, he knew they were idle.

Compare this to the thousands and thousands of women married to alcoholics who say, "If you get drunk ONE MORE TIME, I'm leaving you." And just like the flirting scenario, the threat was never actualized. Why not? Because after she airs her empty threat it relieves some of her frustrations for the moment. For a few seconds, she feels like she has some control back in her life. He acts contrite knowing that her outburst is the WORST punishment he's going to get.

DID SHE HANG IN THERE TOO LONG?

Yes, but that's by the standards of a non co-dependent woman. Every co-dependent woman will hang in there as long as her self-esteem is low and she's too frightened to try to make it on her own. Low self-esteem is behind the kind of misguided thinking that "a bad relationship is better than no relationship at all."

When women finally choose to leave a bad relationship it can be for many different reasons. Some leave because they found another man. Some gain self-esteem through support groups like Al Anon. Some go to work and gain the financial independence to make it without him. Others are beaten to a pulp and leave out of fear for their lives. But no matter how long it takes, when they finally make the break, it's because their self-esteem was heightened through some means. If they had possessed the same self-esteem as when they left, they would have made good on their first threat.

We all have our breaking points. It took years before the woman in the scenario left her marriage. But a woman should never have to suffer abuse for this long. Women have got to find the means to empower themselves so that the fear of being alone doesn't cripple them from taking action. Ask any woman who has left a relationship and you'll probably hear the same words 95% of the time: "I regret that I didn't have the courage to do it sooner." So how do we "empower" ourselves? Through support groups, therapy, a job, and the determination that you are worth a better life than you are living. And when you honestly believe that you are worth more than you're getting, you will be able to walk away from a bad relationship.

#4 THE STONEWALLER

The Scenario:

"I was at a party with my husband. He disappeared for a while amongst the crowd and I didn't think much about it. Then I went into another room (the study) and there he was sitting on the couch next to a friend's wife. He was sort of placing his hand under her chin talking very softly. I couldn't hear what was said. In the next instant when they realized I had come into the room, they broke apart and acted flustered. She immediately got up and left the room. He came over to me attempting to act as casual as possible. He mumbled something about trying to help her with a problem. We left immediately at my request. When I blew up at him and started questioning him, he denied ever having a hand on her face. He said 'You're crazy and you're making a big deal out of nothing.' I told him that I SAW

it with my own eyes, but he stuck to his story that he never had a hand on her. He was merely 'talking' to her about some problem.

I just can't get over his reaction. Does he think that I'm so stupid that I can't trust my own eyes? Does he think he can convince me I was having a hallucination?"

IF YOU DON'T ADMIT IT—IT NEVER HAPPENED

His reaction is commonly known as "stonewalling." It is a classic defense mechanism used by many people who are "caught in the act." The reasoning behind this is that if they never admit to it, they won't have to accept any responsibility for their actions. He put the doubt on his wife hoping she'd start to question what she saw. Then he counted on the tactic of stonewalling long enough for it to all blow over.

Yes, it's a cowardly tactic. But it works for a lot of people. And this guy is going to go to his grave never admitting the truth.

WILL IT ALL BLOW OVER?

He's counting on it. It's up to her to decide if she's going to let this instance go by without further discussion. She may decide to wait and see if he ever does it again and then nail him the next time.

If you ever find yourself facing a situation like this, one thing is for sure, you should never back down on what you saw. You must tell him that you believe, beyond a doubt, that he's lying to you. You also need to add that your trust in him has been seriously undermined. After you have discussed the incident with him, you may come to the conclusion that it was an isolated incident. If so, then you'll need to put it behind you and move on. But, if it is followed by a second incident, you'd be a fool to delude yourself into accepting the same explanation. If you do, you may be in for a lifetime of repetitive behaviors which will ultimately lead to the undoing of your marriage.

What options are open to you?

1. If you catch him cozying up to another woman again, you can confront him on the spot. You should say something like, "What's going on here? You two look awfully chummy." This way, he won't be able to get out of it later by trying to convince you that he wasn't doing what you saw him doing. It also tells him that you're not going to run away with your tail between your legs. You've caught him in a compromising position and you will not give him the opportunity to place you on the defensive. Confrontation will also embarrass

him in front of the other woman and make him think twice about pulling a stunt like this again.

2. When you're dealing with a second offense don't go into denial. He's establishing a pattern of behavior which indicates a clear interest in other women. You're going to have to get to the bottom of it by asking some hard questions. You'll have to find out what he thinks is so unfulfilling about your relationship that he's seeking female attention elsewhere. If he keeps stonewalling and won't tell you what he's really feeling, tell him you're unwilling to leave it at that. Explain your position by saying, "Look, this isn't good enough for me. We've got a BIG PROBLEM between us, whether you're willing to admit it or not. I am going to insist that if we can't resolve this between us, we'll have to seek counseling to resolve it. This is the second time I've caught you doing it and believe me, there isn't going to be a third."

You couldn't be any more clear that you mean business. You are not going to allow him to shrug it off as nothing. You've given him some options, so now it's up to him to decide which remedial course to take.

#5 MULTIPLE PERSONALITY MAN

The Scenario:

"My husband and I spent 45 minutes riding to a restaurant in total silence—which is often typical of the level of communication we share. We've been married for twenty years and I'd bet we haven't had a good, long conversation for about ten of them. Anyway, when we were seated and the waitress came over, all of a sudden 'Mr. Silent' was transformed into 'Mr. Bubbling Personality.' He talked to this babe like she was the most wonderful human being in the entire civilized world. He joked, laughed, teased, and lavished her with compliments. I came 'this close' to shoving the cream pie in his smiling face!"

FROG OR PRINCE?

It seems like there are a lot of wives in this world who have to suffer with "Mr. Silent," while the "Prince Charming" personality is saved for the rest of the female population. Then these clueless men wonder why their wives become increasingly resentful of them. The question that arises in my mind is whether these men are actually AWARE they are exhibiting a dual-personality behavior. I'm sure that once you call it to their attention, most of them will respond by saying, "Well, you never talk to ME either."

What usually happens is this behavior becomes self-perpetuating. A lot of married couples confess that they have run out of things to say to each other. So, instead of either one of them making an effort, they sit in silence. Subsequently, the man feels neglected and expresses this neglect by becoming overly personable with other women out in public. This infuriates the wife. So out of "principle" she won't make an effort to draw him out anymore. This goes on for years until it becomes a moot point as to who started ignoring who first.

HOW TO GET PRINCE CHARMING TO APPEAR FOR YOU

THE WIN-WIN APPROACH: When this situation becomes such a sore point that it's affecting your entire relationship, then it's time for you to take the first step. At this point, it doesn't matter who's being the clueless one. The important thing is that the situation needs some remedial work. So the next time you're together, take the responsibility for initiating a conversation. Start with current affairs. Lord knows there's enough juicy stuff happening in the real world to discuss. Ask his opinion on the current "trial du jour," or about politics, or the sure-to-make-him-blabber topic—sports. If you make it a point to engage him in conversation and ask his opinion on various topics, he's GOT TO TALK to you. Most men LOVE to spout their opinions on every subject imaginable. It's flattering for anyone to be asked their opinion. It means you have respect for their intelligence and an interest in what they have to say. If you take this route, you'll find that you can actually get a dialogue going between you.

It doesn't matter that you're the one who initiates the conversation. Your goal is to resurrect the art of conversation between you. We all know that marriage is one big compromise. So here's your chance to set aside your feelings of resentment in exchange for the "bigger picture"—resolving the communication problem between you.

CLASSIC CLUELESS QUIPS:

#1 "It's okay if he makes an ass of himself at parties. But he expects you to always act like a lady. He won't laugh at your jokes, but he will laugh at another woman dancing on the table—and maybe even join her!"

#2 "When going out with his softball buddies and their wives, he acts like Mr. Personality. When you plan a party with your friends and acquaintances, he is silent, boring, and a real JERK."

Clueless About Family Matters

FAMILY PROBLEMS

The dynamics of a marriage are rarely confined to two people. The relationship is affected by children, in-laws, and a host of other relationships. And ultimately, this blending of people with their own personalities and points of view will bring about joys as well as problems throughout your lives. Knowing this, the most important thing to keep in mind is that old "big picture." As husband and wife, you both share the responsibility of maintaining harmony and stability within the family as well as between yourselves. Quite a juggling act! But it's the area where parents spend the most time and energy.

If you ask married couples what they fight about most, nine times out of ten, they'll say it's either money or their kids. Throw in the in-laws for good measure and you have the potential for thousands of problems to arise over the years. It is crucial for a husband and wife to work out these problems together. Remember that a united front is always the strongest way of dealing with any situation.

Because the "family" encompasses so many different individuals, I have presented scenarios dealing with each of several representative family members.

#1 HOW COULD HE NOT KNOW?

The Scenario:

"I have been married for five years to a man who has two daughters from a previous marriage. They are both in their mid-twenties. One of the daughters is married, the other is single. The single daughter lives alone and doesn't date. She wears mannish clothes and has a 'girlfriend' of several years who visits from another town on weekends. They go to movies, dinners, and vacation together like a couple would. She acts like this is a normal friendship and my husband BUYS it, but I don't. I know she's a lesbian. He acts as if she were totally heterosexual and discusses the girlfriend as if she were a regular friend. From time to time, he casually mentions that he wishes she would find a man and get married. But he never talks about the fact that she might be gay or that the girlfriend situation is at all odd. All of our friends have alluded to me that they think she's gay, but I play dumb because I don't want to stir up a hornet's nest.

How could he be so clueless? It honestly doesn't matter to me in the slightest what her sexual preference is, but I find his total denial of the situation ridiculous. I've thought about telling him that he needs to accept the fact that she is not heterosexual and get out of his denial. But then I always come back to the decision to leave well enough alone."

SHOOTING THE MESSENGER

I think that most of us would agree that in his heart-of-hearts the husband has to suspect that his daughter is involved in a homosexual relationship. The clues are too blatant. And yes, he's in denial. This is a situation that he obviously is unable to cope with so he has taken the path of total denial in his behavior.

The wife has chosen the wisest course, which is to remain silent on the topic. We have all heard the old saying about "shooting the messenger." If she is the one to bring her suspicions up to him or flatly announce that his daughter is gay, she will make herself the target of his wrath. The husband will always resent her forcing him to face a situation he wasn't ready to accept. However, I don't think she's being honest when she says it doesn't bother her. It must or she wouldn't be making such a big deal about it. So far, the husband has ignored talking to his daughter about it because he doesn't want to confront her when she's not comfortable to openly admit it. He probably figures that he would convey his negative feelings about the relationship to his daughter, adding to the burden that she's already carrying. Since she has never approached her father we can assume that she isn't ready to reveal her lifestyle.

The wife has made an intelligent decision not to open up this "can of worms." If faced with the same situation, you've got to ask yourself this question: "What possible benefit would revealing the daughter's lifestyle provide for anybody else?" Remember, it's her life and her choice. The issue of revelation is the business of the father and daughter only. It would do no possible good for the wife to force any revelations from either party. It is not affecting their life as a married couple in any way other than having to dodge some questions from people who don't have the right to ask anyway.

#2 THOSE OLD EX-WIFE BLUES

The Scenario:

"My husband's ex-wife will not leave us alone. She calls at all hours with 'manufactured' problems about their kids. Then she manipulates the kids into tearful scenes with him to try to keep insinuating herself into our lives. His kids call asking for money and complaining about everything, making him feel guilty because he has a happy life now. She is the force behind every unpleasant call and incident he has to put up with.

We have gotten into big arguments over this on countless occasions. I tell him that his ex is behind every move the kids make, but he remains totally clueless. Although he admits that she does make up things to call him about, he insists that the kids are acting out of real concerns of their own. He's in such denial! The kids are in their teens, not little tykes. I wish he would just face reality and stand up to his kids and his ex instead of allowing them to manipulate him."

THE "NOT SO HIDDEN" AGENDA

One of the hardest things in the world to accept is that we have absolutely NO CONTROL over somebody else's behavior. Many people believe that by outsmarting, out-manipulating, and out-scheming the other person, they can bring more peace into their own lives. The truth is that most of these machinations are an exercise in futility. We may win an occasional battle, but generally end up losing the war. Why? Because people act out of their own feelings and motivations, not by how we expect them to.

What is apparent in this scenario is that the ex-wife has her own agenda. It includes bitterness, vindictiveness, and an overwhelming need to keep her ex feeling guilty. She does not want him to enjoy a minute's peace in his new life. It's also obvious that his ex-wife hasn't moved on with her life. She has chosen to stay stuck in destructive patterns, using her kids as pawns in a personal war against her ex.

WHERE THE REAL POWER LIES

The husband is, I believe, not at all that clueless about what his kids are trying to do. However, he is obviously very guilty about not being a full-time Dad anymore. This is what lies behind his reluctance to confront them. He feels safe unleashing his anger on his ex-wife because there is no emotional commitment between them anymore. But he will always have a bond with the kids and he doesn't want to do anything that might alienate that bond. It's also very difficult for him to come to grips with the reality that his kids are manipulating him. It's very painful for anyone to admit they are being "played for all they can get" and practically impossible when it's your own kids. Unfortunately, in many divorce situations, the kids learn that manipulating their parents through guilt gets the results they're seeking. Younger kids as well as teenagers learn to "play one parent off the other" to get what they want. It's a common pattern of behavior which happens when "warring parents" are attempting to "win the kids over" to their own side. This is one of the many distasteful repercussions of divorce and it happens all too frequently.

You must go back to the premise that you can't change anyone else's behavior—his included. All you can do is explain that you feel his ex-wife is prompting at least some of the discontent the kids are exhibiting. Hopefully, it will sink in enough for him to stop feeling guilty after every call from the kids. What you CAN CONTROL, however, is how YOU react to the problem. You are well aware that the ex is trying her best to cause trouble between you and your husband. You've got to remember the old "big picture," which is a loving relationship with your husband. You cannot allow his ex-wife's manipulations to arouse so much anger in you that it's going to cause unnecessary fights between you and your husband. Once you do, you're allowing his ex to control your life. YOUR REACTIONS are making it possible for HER to win. You must always keep this in mind.

#3 DREDGING UP THE PAST

The Scenario:

"Whenever my husband and I are visiting with his mother, she never fails to bring up his old girlfriends in the conversation. The woman can't

remember what she had for breakfast, yet she remembers every one of her 'Sonny Boy's' dates in full detail going back 30 years. She'll say things like, 'Remember how crazy you were about Sally? She sure looked gorgeous in that strapless pink gown the night you two went to the prom.'

Or else she'll say things like, 'Whatever happened to that girl you went with back in the 70's? You know—what's her name? The pretty one with the long blond hair. Do you ever hear from her?'

Then there's always 'Remember the vacation to Brazil you and Dad and I went on when you were married to Katherine? That night in that little bistro was something!! Remember how we all danced until dawn?'

To make matters worse, my clueless husband sits there grinning and shaking his head like some puppet from the 'Howdy Doody Show.' What an idiot! It's so rude. Sometimes I think they're deliberately ganging up on me to try and make me feel like an outsider. I always leave my in-law's feeling hurt, furious and like I'm a nobody."

JUST WHAT IS HER POINT?

Obviously, the husband and the mother are getting some sort of "jollys" from reliving the good old days. His mother may be trying to:

1. Make you jealous so you'll appreciate her son more by using the tactic of keeping you just a bit insecure at all times.
2. Or maybe it just makes her feel younger to relive the past when her son was a bigger part of her life.
3. Possibly, the mother and new wife haven't had enough time to bond like she did with the ex-wife.

The husband may go along with his mother because:

1. He doesn't want to make her feel bad by quashing her memories.
2. He also likes keeping you a bit insecure by periodically reminding you that there were other women in his life. In some twisted way, he probably thinks this will keep you from taking him for granted. If he frequently makes references to women in his past when he's away from his mother, then this explanation probably fits your situation.

But whatever their individual motivations are a steady diet of this kind of talk is very inconsiderate.

WHO DO YOU TALK TO?

This is actually a problem between the wife and her husband. Even though his mother initiates it, it probably wouldn't be wise for the wife to directly confront her mother-in-law. She needs to speak directly to her husband about it. I would make it clear to him that his willingness to engage in conversation about old girlfriends with his mother is only encouraging her to do it more. He needs to be told that these "reminiscences" serve only to hurt you, make you uncomfortable and feel left out. The wife should appeal to her husband's sense of fair play. She should say, "Honey, when you and your mother are dredging up past girlfriends, there's no way I can contribute to the conversation. I wasn't there, so I have no way of including myself. These conversations have no relation to me and only serve to exclude me."

Then it's up to him to speak to his mother on his wife's behalf. He could say something like, "Mom, I would appreciate it if you don't bring up all my old girlfriends in front of my wife. She has confided to me that it really hurts her feelings. She cares for you too much to make an issue of it, so I am asking you. You can discuss these things when we're alone, but please don't bring it up in front of her anymore."

If his mother still does it, then he will have to take the next step. He will have to admonish her again, but this time in your presence. This will give his position a double impact.

If they BOTH still continue these little discussions, then you have every right to interrupt and tell them how uncomfortable they're making you feel. Or, if worse comes to worse, you should get up and leave the room to make your discomfort perfectly clear. Unless the mother and son are totally "clueless" this action should make the point and get them to stop doing it in your presence.

#4 WEIGHTY PROBLEM

The Scenario:

"We have a problem with our daughter which my husband's behavior is making worse by the day. Emily is 14 and overweight. I am constantly monitoring her diet and encouraging her to exercise. I am trying to help her control her weight by using every positive method I can. My husband, however, badgers her constantly. He's always making 'fatty' remarks or unkind 'piggy' jokes in an attempt to shame her into losing weight. I know it's hurting her immensely and she probably sneaks food behind our backs to try and assuage her hurt. His unkind behavior is the source of daily

arguments between us. Emily never says anything to him because she is a
sweet, passive kid. I have tried telling him in every way possible to 'cool
it' with her and that his berating is going to force her into gaining even
more weight. How can he be so cruel? I have such resentment for the way
he continues to disregard her feelings. It's driving a wedge between the
whole family."

A FAMILY PROBLEM

There are several aspects to this situation that come to mind immediately.
The first concerns the husband's inappropriate behavior. It is always wrong to
try to motivate another person through belittling and abusive behavior. And
this is exactly what this man is attempting to do.

The second aspect is that this problem is a total family problem. It is causing resentment between the husband and wife, as well as between the husband and daughter. And even though the daughter remains silent, you can be
assured that she resents the father's cruelty in his interaction with her.

The third aspect is with the daughter, herself. The weight gain could be
from a medical problem, an emotional problem, or both. The root cause or
causes must be ascertained before remedial action is attempted.

INTERVENTION

The entire family needs to be in counseling to stop the cyclical damage being
done by the husband. A competent counselor needs to meet with the family
as a unit to begin correcting the damage already done. The husband is obviously not listening to his wife nor understanding the validity in what she's
saying about the negative way he's handling their daughter. Therefore, an out-
side authority needs to intervene. The father must have counseling for whatever time it takes to make him realize the damage he's doing and what steps
he must take to correct it.

The daughter should be taken to an internist or an endocrinologist who
can ascertain if there is a medical reason behind her obesity. This might
include a thyroid test or whatever he deems necessary to get to the cause of
her weight gain. And if there is a physiological cause, the girl still needs counseling to restore her bruised self-image. This child has suffered enormously at
the hands of her father and will require counseling to restore her self-esteem.

The husband and wife also need counseling to help heal the wounds of
resentment his behavior has caused between them. The counselor will work
with the family, as a whole, to teach them how to resolve their problems using

love and kindness instead of anger. As it stands now, the situation is completely destructive to everyone in the family.

Also, the husband needs to explore the reasons for his hostility towards his daughter through counseling. He must be taught how to handle people with love. He is an abuser of the worst kind—abusive to a child. To a child, mental abuse can be just as harmful as physical abuse. And this cycle must be stopped by the mother's intervention. Almost every parent goes overboard in remonstrating a child now and then. But when a person is exhibiting ONGOING ABUSIVE BEHAVIOR towards a child, immediate counseling is a MUST.

#5 THE OLD DOUBLE STANDARD IS ALIVE AND WELL

The Scenario:

"We have two teenagers, a 16-year-old daughter and a 17-year-old son. Both go to the same high school, are good students and very popular. My husband is still tuned in to the 'good ole boy' philosophy of life. He allows our son to stay out until all hours on weekends, gave him his own car, and encourages him to date and 'have fun' (we all know what that means). When it comes to our daughter, however, the rules are dramatically different. She has a 12 o'clock curfew and he grills her unmercifully about her dates. He also never acts politely to any of them. He lets her know, in no uncertain terms, that if she is sexually active, she's dead. Naturally, she resents the tough line he takes with her while drawing no line where her brother is concerned. And frankly, so do I. His excuse is that boys are going to 'do it' anyway, but he won't stand for having a promiscuous daughter. My daughter and I find his attitude obnoxious and unfair. Our son blows it off by saying, 'Dad's just acting like a typical ol' man.' But I say the ol' man is clueless about how to raise children."

AND JUSTICE FOR ALL

The husband's attitudes are archaic. He needs to be made aware that we are living in dangerous times—that sexual promiscuity is wrong for BOTH boys and girls. Besides the obvious fact of AIDS being out there, the whole idea of sleeping around for guys as being "natural" is a load of bull. It's important that boys of any age be taught to RESPECT women. Condoning promiscuous behavior by saying "boys will be boys" is a big cop-out! Both boys and girls need to be taught in the home, at an early age, that sex only has a place in a loving, committed relationship. No human being has the right to "use" another for his or her personal gratification.

SO WHO SHOULD REEDUCATE THE MAN?

Unfortunately, the attitudes of the husband are being passed on to the son, who will ultimately raise his kids the same way. If the husband will not listen to the reasoning of his wife and daughter, they will have to put him in touch with someone who can make him see things in the correct light. This would be the role of an independent family counselor, a psychologist, or clergyman. The father needs to be educated as to the "bigger picture." And that bigger picture is the whole area of human rights. This is not going to be an easy job. The husband's attitudes are steeped in generations of misogyny. It will require an authority figure, who he highly respects, to persuade him that his attitude desperately needs changing. Anything less will fall on deaf ears. And in this situation, the mother cannot rest until she finds someone who will be able to reach her husband and change his behavior. The future well-being of those kids is going to be ultimately decided by the ability of someone to talk some sense into their father.

Both boys and girls need structure, guidance, and moral teachings from their parents. But it needs to be done equally. The authority figure must convince him that he is giving his son the wrong message. Right now, the message he's giving is that men are inherently superior to women and deserve more God-given rights. In turn, his daughter is being given the message that sex is abhorrent and women are NOT TO BE TRUSTED. If they're not corrected, these messages are going to produce two dysfunctional teenagers who are on the verge of becoming dysfunctional adults.

CLASSIC CLUELESS QUIPS

#1 **"Dad knows he shouldn't set a bad example by leaving the family at the dinner table to watch sports on TV. So he compromises—in order not to miss a single play during dinner, he turns the volume up so loud nobody can talk much less think!!"**

#2 **You've worked all day to make a lovely dinner of creamed chicken. While eating it, he remarks, "Why don't you sell this to the city to fill the potholes on Main Street."**

9

Clueless About Pregnancy

WHEN YOU CAN'T SWITCH PLACES

We have all heard of the old saying, "Walk a mile in my shoes." It's a darn good one to remember when we're trying to understand someone else's motivations. Unfortunately, there are exceptions—and pregnancy, for obvious reasons, is a big one. Women constantly complain that their husbands are totally clueless about trying to understand them during their pregnancy. And why not? Pregnant women are often clueless themselves about where many of their shifting emotions are coming from. They're happy one minute, crying the next, suffering from indigestion, plagued with stuffed sinuses, and carrying a lot of extra weight around. But all women agree that their temporary discomfort is a small price to pay in exchange for the lifetime of joy their child will bring them.

It is vitally important to keep the lines of communication open with your spouse during pregnancy in light of all the conflicting emotions you are experiencing. It's going to be a time when your sexual patterns will have to change, as well as making adjustments in many other areas of your lives. And the best way to handle it all is to keep your husband informed as to what's going on with you. It will also be a big help if he reads about pregnancy and educates himself about the important aspects you'll be facing together. This way, at least he can deal with you in a much more informed manner. Nowadays, men are much more into the whole birthing process than they were a decade or more ago. They attend LaMaze classes, are present in the delivery room, and sometimes even help in the birthing process. Thankfully, men are no longer treated as outcasts and left alone to pace the floors of the waiting room.

#1 SEX TAKES A BACK SEAT

The Scenario:

"I am in my sixth month of pregnancy. I'm tired, bloated, and generally uncomfortable all the time. My husband is acting in the most clueless way possible. He gets upset when I'm too tired for sex and just doesn't understand that I don't feel sexy anymore. He sulks like a two-year-old and makes these idle threats that he'll have to start looking elsewhere if I can't come across. I wish he could understand what it's like to carry around an extra 40 pounds and try to keep up with life's normal activities during pregnancy. I feel depressed a lot of the time and our relationship has become sort of silent and sulky. I bet if he were the one who was pregnant, he wouldn't feel like having sex for the entire nine months."

GETTING THINGS CLEAR

It is necessary for husbands to be completely informed as to what is going on with their wives, emotionally as well as physically, through each month of their pregnancy. This man would benefit from attending some of her doctor appointments and gain some firsthand information about what his wife's pregnancy is all about. The doctor will be able to explain the physiology of sex during pregnancy and tell him at what point during the pregnancy, if any, intercourse is not advisable. When it's done in this way, he won't always be wondering if you are "making things up" or looking for excuses to avoid him. Things are going to make a lot more sense to him when he hears it from a professional. It will certainly validate what you're trying to tell him.

THE WIN-WIN APPROACH:

In turn, the wife has to be very open about how she feels. She shouldn't feel awkward about telling him that intercourse has become too uncomfortable for her. She should feel free to candidly discuss whatever difficulties she is experiencing without fear of reprisals. But it's most important that she let him know that her reluctance has NOTHING to do with her FEELINGS for him. The basic problem between them has been that he has interpreted her reluctance as an act of rejection. But when he really understands what's happening with her physically, he shouldn't feel rejected any longer. And remember, it's always beneficial to be creative. If intercourse is impossible, then you can be sexual with one another in alternative ways. Touching, oral sex, or any one of a number of different techniques can keep you both close and satisfied.

FURTHER RAMIFICATIONS

Men are naturally going to feel a little scared about the prospect of another mouth to feed. Additionally, there are a lot of husbands who are concerned that once the baby arrives, their wives aren't going to have time for them anymore. And the truth is, to a large extent, this does happen. It's an overwhelming time for a new mother. She will be faced with the continual demands of taking care of a newborn while trying to manage the home and remain an attentive wife. She is being pulled in a hundred different directions.

THE WIN-WIN APPROACH:

In order for the husband to not feel neglected, he needs to be included in all aspects of your new family life. Both parties must realize that this is a new chapter in their relationship which will require enormous compromise. It's a demanding time, but it certainly shouldn't be one of estrangement and abandonment. Both parties need to remember that the marriage needs nurturing as well as the new baby. They should make a special effort to reserve time for themselves. In order to let the husband know he is not being forgotten, you should say something like, "Honey, I know you've had a tough day and I want to spend some time with you. I am going to feed the baby and put him to bed, but afterwards, we'll have a couple of hours for ourselves." This lets him know that you're not overlooking him and are also making the effort to give him some attention. You can choose a video, make a special dinner, or use the time for snuggling and conversation. It's this kind of effort which will allow you to stay as connected and close as you were before the baby came.

#2 DOESN'T WANT SEX ANYMORE AFTER THE BABY

The Scenario:

"After the birth of our first child our sex life dropped off quite a bit. I attributed it to exhaustion, breast feeding, etc. You know—the usual mil-

lions of 'new parent' things that keep you both totally involved. But now, after our second child, I find that my husband really seems to have a thing about not touching me anymore. But he still watches me like a hawk and if another man pays me any attention, he's right by my side fawning all over me. I've tried talking to him, pitching a fit, you name it. I get nowhere. He doesn't want me sexually, yet he seems scared to death someone else might. He doesn't seem to have a clue as to how he feels or what's happening to him. And neither do I."

THE MADONNA SYNDROME

It's amazing how many women have complained about this problem. They wonder if there is some psychological condition which turns men off to sex after their wives have given birth. Is it that men see their partners as a "mother" and not as a wife anymore? Psychologists sometimes refer to this behavior as the classic "Madonna" complex, in which the husband identifies the mother of his children as sort of a mother in general. And because having sex with one's mother is unthinkable, now sex with his wife becomes more and more of a taboo. This particular sexual dysfunction is a lot more common than you might think. But no matter what the cause, the fact remains that this can be a big problem to overcome. I have talked to many women who say that their husbands really don't know why they are behaving this way. When the wives approached them for an explanation they totally denied that they were avoiding their wives sexually. Certainly they must realize that most women are not going to remain in a sexless marriage for very long. But in spite of this possibility, they persist in the behavior—probably because they are unable to change it.

The husband in this story has demonstrated jealousy when other men pay attention to his wife. And why not? He's confused not unconscious. But he's also aware of the reality that if she can't get sex from him, she's eventually going to succumb to another man.

THERAPY

So what should she do? First of all, she has to be very honest about their current situation to get at the true root of his behavior. Did she gain a lot of weight that she hasn't been able to shed? Is she ignoring him and giving all her attention to the baby? In other words, could there be an obvious reason why he is turning off to her sexually? If none of these things are applicable, then she has to assume that he has a serious psychological problem with roots that probably go back a long time.

The wife should insist that they enlist the aid of a therapist who is familiar with this type of problem. It's unrealistic for her to assume that one day he might miraculously resume his sexual desire towards her without an understanding of his deep-seated problem. Very few people can live in a sexless marriage for a long duration. It will eventually destroy their marriage if they don't seek help. But it's encouraging to know that there are thousands of couples with the same problem who have been helped. *The important thing is not to let this situation get to the point where you don't care if the marriage can be repaired or not.*

#3 THE OTHER SIDE OF THE COIN

The Scenario:

"What do you do with a man who is absolutely clueless about our sex life after the baby has come? It's only been four weeks and I simply cannot perform 'on demand' whenever HE feels like it. He doesn't understand that besides my episiotomy being tender, I'm breast feeding, doing a ton of baby clothes in the wash day and night, coping with screwed-up hormones, and constantly fighting exhaustion. He's trying to carry on our sex life just like before we had a baby. I'm trying to lose weight and don't exactly feel great about stuffing my body into a Victoria's Secret mesh teddy! Get the picture? He's all dejected and depressed these days—exactly how I feel. Men should have to deliver an 8 lb. 6 oz. 'bundle of joy' in order to get the real picture about how our bodies are stretched to the max! He's acting like a bigger baby than our newborn."

BABY, OH BABY!

Trying to cope after the baby arrives is, without a doubt, the most frequent complaint of new mothers. This woman obviously is swamped by the enormous amount of demands placed upon her. She's dealing with the demands of a new baby, the continuing demands of being a homemaker, and the physical demands that her post-partum body is placing upon her. To add to all this, the husband's sexual demands also seem to escalate during this time. This woman's story evokes sympathy from all of us who have "been there, done that." There is no easy solution either. It's a time of "trying to please everyone," and the woman has a right to feel overwhelmed.

Is the husband acting like a baby? Yes, he is. But he's acting like most of the male population would under the same circumstances. From his point of view, he's got a lot of insecurities he's dealing with—the top of the list being:

1. His needs will now come second to the baby's.
2. His wife will adopt the persona of "Mommy" and cease to be sexy and spontaneous from now on.
3. His freedom will be curtailed.

Are these fears justified? Well, the bad news is that in many cases they are. Many, many women have told me that for a year or so after the baby came, their interest in sex just dwindled down to nothing. Whether this is because it's a hormonal thing or a psychological thing about being a "mommy" now, is unclear. But it doesn't matter. The important thing is that she's going to have to deal with the problem. And to deal with it, she has to truly sympathize with her husband's feelings. She just can't write it off by saying he's "acting like a baby" and leave it at that. Even if he is, she needs to deal with his fears in order to help him overcome them.

IS IT IMPOSSIBLE?

Once again, when dealing with any situation where there are elements of multi-dimensional problems one must remember the "big picture." Remember, the "big picture" is a loving, nurturing, and happy relationship. And to accomplish it, you'll have to find solutions to keep all of you connected, non-resentful, and happy. And no, I'm not saying that this is all up to the woman. But in the instance of sex, there's only the two of you involved, so this one's "on you" so to speak. Yes, you are tired and feeling like a bloated whale. But in reality, this doesn't mean that your sex life should come to a screeching halt. Once again, it is vitally important for the husband and wife to COMPROMISE on this issue.

Communication is tantamount. He has to be told that it will be impossible to have a sex life exactly as it was before the baby came. The baby's schedule is going to alter your spontaneity—that's a given. It will be more infrequent for a while, but assure him that it won't stop. The most important thing for a husband and wife is to keep bonded by nurturing each other. Without this, you create estrangement and those emotionally isolating barriers are erected forever. Keeping this in mind you can both take steps to insure this doesn't happen to you.

THE WIN-WIN APPROACH:

Some couples work out a dating schedule where they hire a sitter for Friday night, dress up, go out for a romantic dinner and then come home and make love. You both are going to have to put this on a top priority basis. The baby will have your love and nurturing 99% of the time. It's no crime to take a couple of hours out for yourselves to nurture one another. The romantic aspect of your relationship shouldn't stop when the baby arrives.

It's also crucial that a woman keep seeing her doctor on a regular basis. Don't be shy about discussing your sexual problems with him. Doctors are trained to help you with them. He/she has heard it a million times. If intercourse is painful have your gynecologist examine you. There may be a problem with your episiotomy or some other gynecological dysfunction which is easily corrected with medication. Get vitamin supplements to keep your energy up. Get a girlfriend or family member to help lighten your load with the baby if you can't afford help. There are a lot of creative ways to lighten your burden.

I'll tell you what I see an awful lot of with mothers today—and you're probably not going to like it. Time and time again I see women who develop the persona of "Super-Mom." I have seen women who refuse to have a sitter for their child until the child is five or six years old because they feel they "can't trust anybody." They eat, sleep, and obsess on "baby." Then they bitch because their husbands "don't understand." They drag the baby everywhere, even to places where children's presence really isn't appropriate. They bring them to women's luncheons, adult dinner parties, weddings, and worst of all, to bed between themselves and their husbands. Let's face it—this is obsessive. And what ends up happening is that the child dictates everything in the parent's life. And this is not the natural order of things. We can be devoted, loving parents without our children running us. And I think it's obvious that over the long haul, this behavior is extremely detrimental to the child's normal development.

#4 ONE MORE MAKES A LITTER

The Scenario:

"Four years ago, when my husband and I married, we both wanted to have three kids. We have two beautiful boys ages one and three. I have my hands full with both but I'm not really complaining. They are a joy but consume every minute of my time. My husband has decided it's time for the third. However, I've changed my mind. I am completely happy with two and I've decided that's it for me. Now he's very angry and feels I've reneged on my promise. I know I couldn't handle another child without my life turning into chaos. His job is very demanding and he's away so much that I feel like I'm raising these children as a single parent most of the time. I can't

understand why he would even want another when he's pretty much an absentee parent as it is. Besides, he's not the one who has to go through another pregnancy. I'm in my mid-thirties and don't want to be pregnant again.

I think that he's being very selfish and refuses to understand the commitment and work it takes to bear and raise children. I guess he'll cool off in time, but life isn't much fun with him now. I think he is totally out of touch when it comes to the reality of having and raising kids."

WHEN COUPLES DON'T AGREE

There are countless other couples who have run into the same problem. Before you get married it's imperative that you discuss and agree on what size you want your family to be, or even whether or not you want to have kids. A man or woman who does not want to have children and has the courage to admit it should not be looked upon as someone to be scorned. Rather, it's the person who doesn't want them but agrees to it under duress who is the dishonest one. So you must be honest when you discuss the issue of having or not having children. It's smart and practical. BUT—and this is a big BUT—until you actually bear and raise children, both parties are making decisions about something they haven't experienced yet. When you initially make your decision there is no way of knowing if there will be adversities in the future—like a time-consuming job, ill-health, lack of money, or other circumstances—which could force you to rethink your decision. This is why you will need to remain flexible about your previous decisions as your lives evolve over time.

The reality is that it's usually the wife who must assume the lion's share of the work in the day-to-day responsibilities of raising children. There are many people (including myself) who strongly believe that it is totally unfair to bring any child into this world when one or both parties feel that they aren't able to raise it with the necessary time and love that every child deserves. It's not only unfair but potentially the most destructive thing you can do to any innocent child. Too many people subscribe to the theory that "a bad parent is better than no parent at all."

IS IT OKAY FOR THE WOMAN TO SAY "NO"?

There is no right or wrong here. In this scenario, he is somewhat justified in feeling that she went back on a promise. But she has given him valid reasons for her decision not to have any more children. And it's her body and ultimately her right to make this decision.

THE WIN-WIN APPROACH:
Unfortunately, this is a situation where there really isn't any opportunity for compromise. Either they have a baby or not. But if she voices her decision not to have a child, she'll have to cope with his disappointment. In order to do this, she'll need to provide circumstances to show him that their present family status is comfortable for them. For example, she should plan some activities like picnics or camping trips for the whole family to enjoy. She should also plan for some special nights just for the two of them. Then she'll be able to point out the validity of her decision by saying, "Honey, wasn't that a romantic evening? I hope you enjoyed being together as much as I did. You know, if we had a baby, we just wouldn't be able to do these kinds of things anymore." This way, it shouldn't take too long for him to get the message that his present family life is fulfilling and successful. And who can argue with success?

#5 DOES HAVING A BABY CEMENT THE RELATIONSHIP?

The Scenario:

"When we got married six years ago we were both career-oriented individuals. We planned to have children, but never really set a timetable for ourselves. Now after six years I find that our lives are pretty empty. All we have is work and our possessions and frankly, it isn't enough for me anymore. I am completely ready to have a baby. I'm positive that a baby will bring the fulfillment into our lives which is presently lacking. My husband disagrees and says that he 'isn't ready yet'. It's always 'wait until we can afford a home, or a new car, or something else.'

After lengthy discussions, he won't give me any reasons for delaying children other than 'he wants to wait a few more years.' I'm wondering if I should just get off the pill and see what happens. Waiting a few more years doesn't make sense to me. I think he's being selfish and insensitive to how much better our marriage would be if we had a child to raise and love together."

FOLLOW THESE DIRECTIONS CAREFULLY

This situation would be easier to analyze if she had revealed a little more about their relationship as husband and wife. However, there are some definite rules that apply to any couple considering having children. These rules have been expressed by countless women who have been dealing with the same situation for generations:

1. Never bring a child into this world unless both parents are in complete agreement about having the baby.
2. Children will never cement a relationship that is already failing or unfulfilling.

The first rule has been discussed in previous scenarios. Regarding the second rule...

If a relationship feels empty enough to compel one of the parties to fill it up with children, it IS NOT going to work. The problems causing the emptiness are not going to go away by having children. Yes, the children will be a joy and the wife can lavish her love on them, but they will not heal the lack of love between her and her husband. Also, a child can't make them love each other more. It just doesn't work that way. It most likely will do MORE DAMAGE to the marriage because the husband may resent the child he didn't agree to. And then the wife will also feel resentment because she's raising the child with very little help from her husband. This will cause her to lavish all her love onto the child while she grows more indifferent to the needs of her husband.

DEADLINE

It's imperative for a husband and wife to sit down and agree on a plan for the future. If your husband is sincere that he doesn't want a child until some future time, then he should make a solemn commitment as to when that's going to happen. Whether it's one year from now or two, and you agree to it, that promise should be accepted as a sacred one. Naturally, there is a chance that he may agree to this just to "buy time" and then come up with a new set of excuses as the deadline approaches. But, as with any promises you make in a marriage, some things just have to be taken on faith. The only thing you can do when he makes his promise is to tell him that his word means everything to you. Hopefully, if he truly understands that this commitment is tantamount to the future trust you have in him, he won't take it lightly.

If your husband keeps wavering or will not agree to a definite time, then you'll need to go for counseling to see what's behind his hesitation. There may be a lot of unresolved conflicts which need to be worked out between you. Or, it may come out that he is actually equivocal in his feelings about YOU and the child issue is a way of avoiding this underlying reason. There's a lot to be worked through in this situation. Also, if your husband is unsure of his feelings about your marriage, he will view a child as locking him in it forever. And this may be the real reason for his reluctance to have one. Likewise, if you sense his equivocation about his feelings for you, you may use a child as a means of trying to keep him in the marriage. In either case, working out the problems in the marriage should be the priority. Whether or not to have a child is an issue to be decided only after the marriage is on solid ground.

CLASSIC CLUELESS QUIP

"**My water broke at the dinner table one night and it looked like three gallons hit the floor. My husband jumped up—and grabbed ONE napkin to clean it up!!**"

The Financially Clueless

WHAT MONEY REALLY STANDS FOR

If you ask couples what they argue about most, money is always in the top three along with kids and sex. It seems contradictory that even though most of us were raised to believe that money can't buy happiness, it's still considered an important ingredient to be successful in life. But when we get to the root of what money represents, it's actually not a mystery anymore.

Think about it. What is the one thing that money can buy if not happiness? Nowadays, women are finding out the secret men have known for years. It can buy a certain amount of independence. And through this it represents power. A few decades ago our roles were cut and dried. Men made the money and women stayed home with the children. The women who were stuck at home had no real earning power on their own and many increasingly began to realize that they had no independence or power either. So we got smart. Women began working in greater numbers than ever before. Whether inflation forced them to help supplement their husbands' incomes or whatever the reason, their new incomes suddenly gave them a new-found independence their mothers never had. And ultimately, that income meant they no longer were forced to remain in bad marriages. With money in the bank they could provide a roof over their own heads and food for themselves and their children. Having their own money provided them with the ability to make choices previously unavailable to them.

There are several reasons why money is the source of a growing antagonism between the sexes. The power and independence it brings to women frightens a lot of men. Also, if the woman begins earning more than the husband, some men feel emasculated. Then there's the added problems when two people work of who pays for what. Is it fair to live off the husband's salary and bank the wife's? Should each spouse keep their own money in separate accounts? Will the wife's salary only be enough to cover child care expenses with little else left over? When both husband and wife earn money, there will be many issues raised on which they will have to come to terms.

#1 THE ULTIMATE IN CHEAP MEN

The Scenario:

"I'm sure I'm not the first woman who has complained about having a cheap husband. I've suffered for 15 years with this tightwad. My husband has always provided for our children and me so it's not like we've been destitute or anything. But he has always been extremely tight with his money. He hasn't really increased our food and clothing expenses much over the years and he doesn't have a clue about how much necessities cost nowadays. We usually end up fighting because he accuses me and the kids of spending too much money.

We have two teenage girls and you know how much it costs just to keep them in makeup and clothes. The other night he went ballistic when he saw a $350 credit card bill for the girls' clothes. I've told him over and over that none of us are being extravagant, it's just what things cost today. I keep telling him that I need to go out and work to ease problems on all fronts, but he says 'there is no way I'm going to allow you to go to work.' He won't give any solid reasons for his decision and just keeps insisting that I need to stay at home."

TRADITIONAL BREAD WINNERS

This woman finds herself in a situation common to a lot of families where the husband is the sole provider. She did not say how much her husband earns in annual salary, but in a way, it's beside the point of her real problem. In today's society, providing for everything including college for two or more kids requires more money than the average man earns. However, the real issue this woman is dealing with is that of control. It seems to me that his vehemence in denying her the opportunity to work, i.e., "there is NO WAY I'm going to allow you to go to work" suggests a deeper problem. Perhaps her working will force him to give up a good deal of control he now enjoys over her and the girls.

He doles out money in food and clothing allowances but never seems to give enough to adequately cover their needs. Then he screams over what is spent. These are the actions of a man who is using the money to control all of them. He keeps everyone under his thumb with these tactics. As long as he is the only one who is doling out money, it gives him the "right" to have a say about everything they do. And he never lets them forget who they are beholden to either.

GETTING INTO THIS CENTURY

It's time for this woman and a lot of others like her to wake up and see what's really happening. The only way she is going to get out from under his tyrannical controlling power is to go to work herself. Her girls are teenagers and in school most of the day. So it would be possible for her to work from 9 to 5 or part-time without neglecting her motherly duties. Also, it would be a good idea for the girls to get after-school or weekend jobs so they can establish their own level of independence. It will also give them an understanding of the value of a dollar and help them appreciate their father's efforts on their behalf, if they don't already.

 THE WIN-WIN APPROACH:

However, the fact is, she's dealing with an unreasonable husband. And if she takes the "screw you" attitude and goes out and gets a job without his approval, she's going to create even more of a hornet's nest. To achieve the end results she desires—making extra money and establishing some independence—what can she do? She should take a compromising approach by saying, "I know you are against the thought of my getting a job. But I would like to work, part-time, for a trial period of four months. I know the extra money would take a lot of pressure off you and I would still have plenty of time to devote to you and the girls. I also think it wouldn't be a bad idea for the girls to get some work after school or on weekends. This way, they can learn about the value of a dollar and help out too. We can all try it on a trial basis and if it creates problems for you, we can evaluate it and discuss it further at that time. But I think it's important that we at least give it a try."

Another option available to many women in this situation is working at home. There are many companies who hire people to do telemarketing or other sales jobs from their home. Many women are forming their own companies which produce items such as gift baskets, jewelry, or decorating clothing from their homes. Also, if you have a home computer, there are more and more jobs available in which you can create your own flexible hours.

Even if the wife and daughters aren't earning a great deal of money, any amount will still enable them to empower themselves in incredibly beneficial ways. They can help pay for their own clothes, or earn a little extra for occasions like proms or vacations. When they're working hard for their own spending money they'll be a lot less likely to "blow it" on frivolous things. Now their Dad will have a lot less reason to complain. It will alleviate the fighting, the power struggles, and help them to mature. Also, the mother needs to grow up too. For years she has allowed herself to be bullied and controlled by her husband's wallet. She can break the "Catch 22" cycle of being angry with his attitude, but at the same time feeling beholden because he works so hard. Once they are all working it levels the playing field.

In time, if a man has any sense of rationality, he will come to appreciate this economic relief provided by the joint efforts of his family. He may not like it at first, but so what? He can't have it both ways. He can't expect to deny you the right to earn income, but still scream about every dime that you spend.

#2 PAYING FOR THE WOMAN NOT TO WORK

I have heard over a half-dozen stories with the same financial scenario confronting couples who are facing retirement. The following story gives the reader a picture of what's happening frequently in today's economic climate.

The Scenario:

"I have a very good job in an insurance company. I make about $30,000 per year and have held the same job for ten years since the kids went to college. My husband is planning on retiring in six months and has just hit me with this proposition. He doesn't want me to work when he retires. He feels that it will be a great opportunity for us to spend time together, travel, and do all the things we've always said we'd do. I have gotten used to the freedom and independence that my salary gives me. I love going to work and love my life as it is. He has generously offered to pay me half of my salary from his own retirement money if I will quit working.

I'm the one who doesn't have a clue about what to do. I hate to give up the money, the independence, and the pleasure of my work. I'm only 50 years old and I don't feel like I'm ready to be 'put out to pasture' yet. I'm also afraid that if I quit I'll never get another job like this one again because of my age. On the other hand, if I say no to him, I realize I'm being selfish. I know that our retirement years are a time to be shared together. It's the toughest decision I've ever had to make—and I don't know what's the best course to take."

JUDGEMENT CALL

She's right. This is a tough one. There are many women out there who would be thrilled to be paid not to work. However, I'd venture to guess that there would be just as many who would find themselves in the same quandary as this woman. There's so much to be taken into consideration. These are things like the husband's age, what his retirement income will be, and what provisions he has made for the family in case of his death. These are vital issues which must figure into her decision. At 50 years of age, she probably will never be able to duplicate the job or income she has now. She has to make sure that if something happens to her husband and she could no longer secure employment, she and her kids will be provided for adequately. There are too many horror stories about widows who had no knowledge of their husband's financial situation and ended up penniless. And, unfortunately, they were too old to work by the time he passed away. These are the hard financial realities that must be addressed before she should give up her income.

On the other hand, she must consider the ramifications of what he's asking. The retirement could turn into the most wonderful time they have ever experienced as a couple. This marriage will not remain a happy one if he is sitting around all day with nothing to do, waiting for her to come home from work. His idleness and resentment could lead to many potential problems that would ruin their marriage. Keep in mind that this is a possibility, not what's definitely going to happen. However, it is realistic enough to consider when evaluating the whole issue.

FINANCIAL DISCOVERY

As in any other important decision, it cannot be made until the person involved has all the facts at hand. This couple needs to sit down and share all financial knowledge available about their retirement status. This includes monthly income, the kind of life and medical insurance they have, and all other factors affecting their financial status. If she has been convinced that she can stop working with no financial catastrophe in any eventuality, then she'll need to explore her feelings on another level.

THE WIN-WIN APPROACH:

How important is it to her self-esteem and well-being that she keep working? If she truly doesn't want to give up her job there's still a possible compromise that could be worked out between them. The woman might approach her husband and then her boss about the possibility of working part-time. The boss might agree to let her work half-days, every other day, or any other combination. She might have to give up a portion of her medical benefits, but it would be worth it to satisfy the situation. This way, she still gets SOME time in the office and her husband will get to see more of her. Then they can make out a schedule of daily events and trips based on her part-time employment. And if anything should happen to him, she could probably increase her hours again. Also, the entire plan could be attempted on a "trial basis." If it works out to both of their satisfactions then she could continue to work indefinitely. If he is still unhappy with the arrangement after six months or so, then they'll have to re-evaluate and make further decisions.

They'll also have to agree upon what kind of retired life will make them BOTH happy. For some reason, couples in our society don't give much thought to what they really want out of their retirement years. Because we plan so much of our lives before retirement, we probably think that when the stresses of working are gone, we'll be happier not having to make any more plans. However, time on anybody's hands with no way to fill it productively can be DEADLY too. Sadly, there are way too many couples who will tell you that their "golden years" are a nightmare. They have nothing useful to fill their time so they sit around and bicker with each other all day long. By the age of retirement, we should know ourselves, our energy levels, and our interests pretty well. And armed with this wisdom we can plan for the kind of retirement that will bring us the most happiness and contentment.

#3 DIVORCED COUPLES AND MONEY

The Scenario:

"I have recently married a man who, like me, is also divorced. We are both middle-aged with grown kids. We both work. It's a wonderful marriage and we are blissfully happy—except for one nagging problem. He would like us both to pool our individual savings into one joint account. I am opposed to this. We foolishly didn't discuss any of this before we got married. We both

just assumed we would think alike on everything. He got taken to the cleaners in his divorce settlement and you would think that he of all people would know this is not a wise move. Besides, my settlement was substantially more than his present holdings. So I think it would be extremely foolish of me to just hand everything over to him. I'd be much more comfortable if we both kept what we brought into the marriage separate."

TO EACH HIS OWN

This woman's issue serves to illustrate the point that you must discuss crucial financial issues BEFORE the marriage in order to spare yourselves a lot of hard feelings later on. When two divorced people get married there's a lot more financially at stake than if you were two young kids starting out with nothing. Besides the issue of how you're going to handle the monies you each brought into the marriage, there may be the questions about who will be financially responsible for the kids. You must place the same importance on these issues as you would when deciding upon a prenuptial or any other financial agreement which affects your marriage. A lot of women feel it's 'distasteful' to discuss these things and don't want to appear like "goldiggers." But nothing could be further from the truth. It's not only your right but your duty to discuss how you're going to handle previous assets. It's not only in your best financial interest, but also in the best interests of your marriage.

IT'S YOUR CALL

The manner in which finances are managed is strictly an individual choice. Some couples agree to pool all the assets they had prior to their marriage. Others prefer to keep their assets in their own name and pool what is earned from the day of the marriage on. This is generally how assets are handled in states that go under community property law. What you bring into the marriage remains yours unless otherwise stipulated. Everything from the day of the marriage on is considered to be community property and split 50/50 in the event of divorce. No matter HOW you do it, the important thing is that you DO IT IN WRITING before the marriage. It will prevent many misunderstandings and conflicts later on.

#4 I HATE A MAN WITH A SLOW HAND

The Scenario:

"Every time my husband and I go out to dinner with another couple the same embarrassing thing happens. When the waiter places the check on the table my husband never makes the first move to pick it up. By doing this it sort of forces the other guy to say 'Oh, I'll take it. This one's on me.' And then my husband never insists on sharing the check. He willingly lets the other guy pay for it. If the situation arises where the other guy asks my husband for his half, he always pays it. I can't fault him on that. But what really bothers me is that he's never gracious enough to reach for the check first.

He will not admit that his behavior is inappropriate. His only defense is saying he doesn't see 'anything wrong' with letting someone treat us to dinner. I'm sure all our friends think he's a cheapskate. I know I do."

TO REACH OR NOT TO REACH

There's no other way to describe this man. He's not only cheap but his behavior is selfish. She didn't say how long they've been married, but I'm surprised that there are any couples left who are willing to have dinner with them. Men who show a continued reluctance to reach for the tab are not kidding anyone but themselves. It's only a matter of time until all their friends "catch on" to his behavior and they find themselves dining out alone.

TAKING THE BULL BY THE HORNS

This woman has limited options because it's obvious he's not going to change his tactics. If you feel that your husband is a tightwad here's a tactic that just might "loosen" him up: the next time YOU reach for the check. If you're with another couple who has been stuck with the check a few times before, then YOU should offer to treat them to dinner. Or you can tally up the check and inform your husband of the amount you owe. You can bet that he's not going to like it. But nobody likes what he's been pulling either.

#5 HOME IMPROVEMENT?

The Scenario:

"My husband thinks he's Bob Vila. There's only one problem—he doesn't have a clue about how to fix anything. But he's so cheap he insists on doing everything himself. Once, when he tried to fix our dish washer, he flooded the kitchen. Another time he shorted out the wiring in our house when trying to fix an electrical problem. I won't even go into the wallpapering and painting jobs he's screwed up.

He says he does everything himself to save money. But half the time we have to hire a professional to correct the mess he's made. It ends up costing us twice as much in the long run, but this doesn't seem to make any difference to him."

CAN YOU FIX A FIXER?

The "fix-it" kind of guy isn't really motivated by saving money, it's the challenge that's important to him. The fact that it usually ends up costing him twice the normal amount is testimony to that. Building, repairing, nuts, bolts, chain saws, etc.—all of it is a GUY THING. It's what guys are SUPPOSED to do. Right?

THE WIN-WIN APPROACH:

Why deny him the pleasure of fixing or attempting to fix things? At least he's home with you and not off in a bar someplace wasting time. If you're married to a fix-it man, I would suggest that you buy him the series of Time-Life books on repairs and building projects. You might even get interested enough yourself to lend a hand and end up doing projects together. And this way you'll be there to see that the job is done properly! Another idea is to enlist the aid of a seasoned handyman to teach your husband the correct way of doing things. He might be a family member, a neighbor, or a friend-of-a-friend. Now, your husband will have a buddy as well as a teacher to help him with his projects. And if any plumbing, appliance, or electrical problem occurs when your husband is at work and you're at home, quickly call a professional repairman to come and fix the problem before your husband gets home!

CLASSIC FEMALE QUIP

"THE PERFECT HUSBAND is a man who puts no limits on your credit cards, doesn't give you a power drill for your birthday, and let's you talk as much as you want during sex—even if it's long distance."

Clueless Dates

CLUELESS DATES

Dating gives a woman the opportunity to find out how compatible she is with a man and whether or not you both wish to pursue a committed relationship. The truth is that dating can be a bitch. It's about meeting someone and sorting out their good and bad traits—then deciding which one outweighs the other.

One thing you must get clear about is your expectations from the men you are dating. Many women are searching for that "one special man" with whom they can have a lasting, committed relationship. A lot of men are looking for the same thing. But the majority of women feel that there's a lot more men who are just out there for "recreational dating." These are men who have no intention of commitment and are simply looking for good sex, a good time, and no responsibility. This is where women have to get smart. You'll need to identify the intentions of the men you're dating. If you are looking for commitment and find a guy who seems perfect—except for one thing—he's not ready to commit, you must face reality. You are not going to change him by playing games, trying to reel him in, or by any other strategy. And if you think you can, 99% of the time you're going to end up with a broken heart. A man who isn't ready for commitment and tells you so, ISN'T ready. Take his word for it and move on. Seek another man who shares the same goals you do. This is what most of the single women wrote about when they called their dates "clueless." Unfortunately, it's the women who are clueless in this instance.

117

#1 WHAT DO I NEED TO DO—HIT HIM OVER THE HEAD?

The Scenario:

"Hot off the presses, an old beau is coming to town in a week and we agreed to meet for dinner. He just called and announced he plans to stay over at my house (he already has a place to stay with his brother). I said 'Fine, you can sleep on the couch.' I recently made it clear to him that I'm only interested in a committed relationship with the possibility of marriage and kids. And he has stated numerous times that he doesn't want either. But he keeps dropping subtle hints about sex. Why does he think I'd want a quick tumble? Like many men, he has a 'convenient' hearing problem."

WHERE THERE'S EGO THERE'S HOPE

Ah yes, here's a case of the old "lottery principle" in action. If there's a chance in a billion, he's going to make sure he's in the running. This is so typically clueless of men with big egos. By deciding to stay at her home, he obviously feels that his irresistible charm will probably make her give into him, no matter what she previously said.

STICK TO YOUR GUNS

This gal was obviously well-grounded and had a healthy sense of humor about the situation. But women have got to realize that when they make rules for themselves, they have to stick to them in order not to shoot themselves in the foot. In other words, if you want commitment and he has repeatedly said he can't give it to you, then it's your prerogative to either stop seeing him, or say NO to any sexual involvement if you keep dating him. So don't go to bed with him!! If you do, then somewhere deep down, you still believe you can make him change his mind about commitment. And after you have slept with him and realize he still hasn't changed his position, you'll suffer another needless let down.

Just the act of agreeing to let this man sleep on her couch gave this guy hope. He probably thought that she would have insisted that he stay with his brother if she had been 100% sure of her conviction not to sleep with him. But no matter what she had in mind, he got the message that there may be a chance.

The important thing for women to remember is that you do have a choice. But you've got to stick to your guns, gals. You can't have it both ways. A basically uncommitted guy isn't going to reform after a tumble in the hay no matter how great the sex may be. That's YOUR EGO at work here. You have to accept his feelings as gospel and act accordingly. If you give off mixed messages then you're making yourself fair game and setting yourself up for future disappointments. Empower yourself. You should never forget that a committed relationship takes two people agreeing to it of their own free will. A roll in the hay may buy you another weekend, but beyond that, not much else.

#2 WHEN YOU SAY IT'S OK TO DATE OTHERS

The Scenario:

"I have enjoyed many wonderful dating relationships. But it seems like no matter how great we are getting along, at some point they all tell me that it's perfectly all right to date other men. What jerks! I am so sick of hearing it. Why do they feel they have to say this to you? Don't they realize how insulting it sounds? I'd rather that they just keep their mouths shut. It's such a turn-off."

YOU DON'T HAVE TO READ BETWEEN THE LINES

No one ever said that all men get an "A" in diplomacy. But when a man tells you to date others, make sure you hear him loud and clear. What he is really telling you is that he is not ready to make a commitment. So you'd better accept this from the get-go. Don't have any false hopes or illusions. Agreed, it does come out a bit tacky, but give him credit for being honest from the start.

TWO CHOICES

When a man says this to you, you have two simple choices. You can choose to keep dating him and other men too, enjoying the relationships for what they are. Or, if you are looking for commitment, then the wise choice would be to stop dating him. In most cases, a woman who wants commitment but keeps on dating a man who doesn't is going to end up with a crushed ego and a lot of frustration. Women have got to accept the fact that you can't MAKE somebody love you. Constantly trying to win someone over in a relationship is a futile endeavor. You are better than that. You need a man to love you from his own heart and of his own free will. Settling for anything less means that a woman doesn't love herself enough to believe this is what she deserves.

#3 THE BOOMERANG MAN

The Scenario:

"I broke up with a guy about a year ago. It was fairly amicable, but he still calls me and shows up at my house several times a week. It's not like he's stalking me or anything but he just won't get the message that it's over. I've told him to find a girl who really cares about him but he just keeps coming back. He says he can't find anyone he cares about like me. I still occasionally date him as a friend but he just doesn't get the message that I'll never end up with him permanently."

BREAKING THE TIES

The first thing that strikes me about this situation is that the girl did not make much of an effort to end the relationship completely. And because she isn't in another committed relationship herself, I suspect that she likes having him around to "fill in" until she does meet "Mr. Right."

The bottom line is—if women want men to play fair they must do the same. And it is not fair to keep a guy hanging around because there's nothing better out there at the moment. If a man is that stuck on a woman, or vice-versa, it's up to the other party to be honest and tell them unequivocally that it's over. Keeping a man dangling is toying with his emotions and really a very insensitive thing to do. I'd be willing to bet that if a new boyfriend came on the scene and insisted she sever ties with the old boyfriend, the old boyfriend would be history in a heartbeat.

ASSESSING WHAT YOU WANT

Again, if one person is seeking a commitment and the other can't give it, it's a waste of time to keep the relationship going. But you need to be honest about what you want. And not just honest with yourself, but with the other person as well. The kind of chemistry between two people that makes sparks fly IS THERE or it ISN'T. It's just not something you can MAKE happen. So keep your minds as well as your eyes open, gals. You'll avoid a lot of heartache by facing the situation without some unrealistic romantic vision clouding your reasoning. See it for what it is—not what you want it to be.

#4 TROUBLE TELLING THE TRUTH

The Scenario:

"I dated a man steadily for about a month. He told me he was the VP in a marketing firm, earned over $120,000 a year, and owned his own home. He also said that he had been divorced twice. We really had a great time together and we had a lot in common. While I liked the fact that he was successful it truly wasn't the main reason I was so attracted to him. After a month, I found out through mutual friends that he was one of about ten VP's in the firm, made half the amount he originally said, rented not owned his home, and had been divorced three times.

I am no longer seeing him and it's not because he isn't rich or a big-shot executive. It's because he was so deceitful to me. I knew if he was like that in the beginning it was only going to get worse. I simply cannot understand why a man would be so dense as to lie about things that he must realize will eventually come out. Don't men know that women are more concerned with a man's <u>integrity</u> than about how much money he has?"

WHY MEN LIE

First of all, this woman is to be congratulated for a very wise and open-minded assessment of this man. She realized that it wasn't important WHAT he had, but rather WHO he was. And, unfortunately, he turned out to be dishonest. But to her credit, she had the courage to face it and move on despite her obvious attraction to him.

There are those who would argue that he was just trying to "build himself up" so he'd look more successful in her eyes. And this is probably why he acted this way. He was intentionally misrepresenting what he had materially because he obviously felt that this is how women judge a man. He had trouble accepting himself for who and what he was. But the crux of the matter is that he *lied* to her. And any woman who saddles herself with a liar is in for a lifetime of heartache. She will quickly lose all respect for him and respect for herself. And the relationship will go downhill from that minute on. She will never be able to trust him because she has learned that his word means nothing.

The woman in this scenario wondered why men don't realize they'll eventually be caught in their lies. Well, that's the nature of the disease. Liars don't think about consequences. Many truly believe they won't ever get caught. And if they do, they think they'll be clever enough to think up another ruse to cover the last lie. It's not only sick behavior, but it's irrational and destructive, too.

HONESTY IS THE ONLY POLICY

My mother always told me that the only thing you really have in this world worth anything is your word. And as I go through life, these words take on a deeper meaning. Unless you can go to the bank on what someone has to say, everything else about them is meaningless. Relationships have got to be built on this principle. We should write this down *in bold letters* and read it every-day to keep reminding ourselves that it is the first criterion for entering into any relationship. Young girls should be instilled with this philosophy when they begin dating. They have to be empowered with enough self-respect to never settle for anything less in a man. And if they find out he isn't true to his word, he should be declared history.

How many miserable marriages and relationships do we know firsthand or see on talk shows where the women are crying, outraged, and devastated because they have been betrayed by a man who has continually lied to them? And their only defense for remaining with him is that they thought he would "change." We've got to get our heads out of the sand. No man or woman who chronically lies is going to change without intensive therapy—and even then probably not much. You've got to think of a liar in the same category as an alcoholic or abuser. They have a very serious character defect which is going to be extremely difficult to deal with.

#5 LOSERS

The Scenario:

"It seems like every man I've dated for the past few years turns out to be a loser. They either have alcohol problems, can't succeed in their career, or just want sex without commitment. I'm beginning to feel like there are no decent men out there. I'm only 30 and already I'm skeptical about my chances of ever finding a responsible man. I'm also beginning to wonder if it's just ME and if I'm being too picky or unrealistic. Are all the single guys left out there this hopeless? Help."

STANDARDS

It is not at all unrealistic to avoid involvement with a man or a string of men who carry a lot of baggage. When you consider that marriage is a life-long commitment, you are right to keep looking until you find someone who fulfills what you expect in a partner. Naturally, no human being is without some faults or problems. But it's up to you to decide whether these are problems you can cope with or ones that will just get worse with time.

Speaking for those of us who have had a few marriages under our belts, I can tell this girl a few things that will give her some insight. To get involved with a man who has alcohol problems, problems telling the truth, or problems holding down a job, on a *continuing* basis, is getting involved with the WRONG man. These are the kinds of problems which will eventually destroy a relationship. You will spend a lifetime trying to correct the miseries they generate. It is a waste of time that would be best spent finding an emotionally healthy man.

Her story is not at all unusual. In fact, it seems to be the most prevalent complaint voiced by single women who are dating. But take heart. There are a lot of wonderful men out there. But it may take a while to find the right one. The important thing for any woman in this situation is to stop doubting her own standards. It shows a healthy sense of self-worth and maturity to never settle for less than you think you're worth. To do so is selling yourself short and will ultimately lead to an unhappy life. Temporarily having no relationship is better than enduring a bad one for a life time.

PRACTICAL ADVICE

This woman didn't say in her letter, but I wonder where she is meeting these losers? As I read her complaint the following questions about her arose in my mind. Why does she keep attracting this element? Are the "losers" hitting on her because she projects an image of having low self-esteem? Or is she finding men in places that are notorious hang-outs for losers? I think a lot of women will agree that one place NOT to look for a potential life mate is in a bar. Too many men who hang around bars have drinking problems or are mostly interested in one night stands.

So the age-old question is where do you go to meet a decent man? Well, there is no one magical answer. Some women have met future husbands through church social groups, groups like Parents Without Partners, at work, on vacations, social clubs, the supermarket or through reliable friends. And let's face it, when you can meet a man through friends who can vouch for his good character, it eliminates the trial and error of haphazardly dating men you know absolutely nothing about.

There is one piece of practical advice I have heard from single friends that I want to pass on to my readers. When they are having a first date with a man they know literally nothing about, they should always take their own car and meet him in a very public place. One reason for doing this is to provide you with your own means of escape if he turns out to be a colossal bore or just not a "nice" person. But more importantly, at any age, you can never be too careful. It is a sad statement about the world we live in, but too often an accurate one. Men that women meet through dating services or ads in the back of magazines can be risky. Never put yourself in jeopardy. Think ahead and remember that in dating situations, you are responsible for taking care of yourself. So be cautious and ALWAYS TRUST YOUR INSTINCTS.

#6 SEX AND DATING

The Scenario:

"I have to vent my anger about men who expect sex on the first date. It's astounding how many men today feel no qualms about asking for sex on the very first date. And if you say no, 99% of the time, they never call you again. What gives with these guys? It makes a woman feel totally worthless. Can't guys figure out how obnoxious they're being? Don't they know how degraded a woman feels when she realizes that all she represents to them is a piece of meat? I wish they'd all stay home with their blow-up dolls and quit bugging women. Even if they think they're being subtle about it, they aren't. Any woman with half a brain can see through their little charades."

TODAY'S MORALS

This scenario represents the sad-but-true statement about the standards in today's society. The basic reason men behave this way is that, unfortunately, there must be plenty of women out there who are willing to have sex on the first date. And when you don't comply they just move on to somebody else who will. There are many women who are engaging in sex on the first date because they feel it will keep the guy coming back. And it probably will—but only until the guy gets bored and starts seeking a new conquest. Women need to understand that if they choose this behavior, the guy will be coming back only for more sex and not for a long-term commitment. There are always exceptions, but most cases have proven this to be the rule. Women need to have enough self-esteem to demand that there is mutual caring, respect, and a realistic chance for a long-term commitment before she makes the decision to add sex as part of the relationship. In following this course the woman will best protect herself from getting involved in a futile relationship. Rarely will immediate sex lead to a healthy, committed relationship.

Women need to ask themselves the following questions before deciding to have sex on the first date:

"Why am I choosing to have such an intimate experience with someone

I've known for only a few hours?"

"Is there a reasonable possibility that I could get AIDS from a man whose lifestyle I know little or nothing about?"

"Do I want to have sex on the first date for pure physical gratification, or do I think it will keep the guy interested in me?"

"If I go to bed with him on the first date, will he wonder if I do it with everyone else I date? If so, will it bother him?"

"Does he have sex with every girl on the first date?""

"Will I honestly think of myself and my body as a precious, worthwhile commodity afterwards?"

"Is sex without true caring and commitment a meaningless act that will only make me feel more emotionally empty?"

The fact is, if a woman is old enough to be having sex, then she will be making her own decisions about what she expects to get out of it. However, I hope that if you find yourself contemplating sex on the first date, you will honestly answer the questions posed and act according to your better judgement.

CHOICES

Every woman has the right to say "no" to sex on the first date or the hundredth date. If he doesn't call back, it tells you he was not interested in you as a person, but rather as a means to his own gratification. And nobody wants to be or should allow themself to be used for someone else's gratification. If a person does, it's usually the result of low self-esteem.

Fortunately, there are still a good deal of men out there who don't expect sex right away. These are men who truly respect women and care enough about them to wait until the relationship shows definite signs of exclusivity and of lasting, before introducing sex into the mix. When should you have sex? After the fifth, tenth or fiftieth date? Again, there are no patent formulas to follow. But when both parties reach a point where there is a healthy respect and caring between them, and they feel secure about their feelings for each other, then the time is right for a sexual relationship. Sex accompanied with love and commitment will be bonding and fulfilling. When one or both parties accepts anything less, they're going to feel empty and cheated.

TACKY BEHAVIORS OF CLUELESS DATES

- Men who don't go even slightly out of their way to do anything special for your birthday.

- Men who think common courtesies, (like holding the door open for you) are for "wimps!"

- Men who promise to call you the next day and then wait a week so they won't appear "too interested."

- Men who prefer that a woman doesn't have strong opinions on anything.

- Men who want to go "dutch" on every date.

- Men who take you out for an expensive evening and then expect to be reimbursed with sex.

- Men who always hog the conversation, interrupting you at every opportunity.

- Men who chain smoke for that "rugged" look.

- Men who are habitually late because it makes them seem "cool."

- Men who refuse to use condoms because they claim it spoils THEIR sexual enjoyment.

- Men who constantly brag about their sexual prowess, but don't know the first thing about how to bring a woman to orgasm.

- Men who don't wear deodorant because they think their natural body odor is an "aphrodisiac."

EPILOGUE

In the process of determining what kind of advice I was going to give in answer to the scenarios I consulted a number of men for their opinions. I felt that it would be helpful in order to keep the content from becoming too "one-sided." It's very easy to fall into the trap of thinking, "Well, the guy is totally at fault in this scenario. Why should the woman have to compromise?" However, in a relationship, it almost becomes immaterial as to who's right and who is wrong. The important thing to remember is that the goal of any relationship should be to make each other happy, secure, and to continually nurture one another with love. This is what I mean when I constantly refer to the "Big Picture." And to achieve it, there has to be a great deal of compromise by BOTH the man and the woman.

I believe that most of the common, day-to-day problems which arise in a relationship can be resolved through compromise. Granted, it's not always going to be a 50/50 proposition. Many times, one partner will have to "give in" more than the other. But as long as each person feels like they've gained SOMETHING without having to give up EVERYTHING, you've made a successful compromise. It's called a "win-win" proposition and it's the goal to aim for whenever you're working through a problem. I've tried to follow this principle when giving advice.

It's important for women to understand that lecturing, nagging, or just TELLING the man he is wrong, will generally not get the result you're looking for. In most cases, placing blame leads to a "dead-end" street. It is incredibly difficult to change another person's behavior simply by telling him that he's wrong. But we can change how we react to and how we handle a problem. We have to start thinking in terms of finding solutions acceptable to both partners.

Unfortunately, there are always those cases in which a person is so dysfunctional that the only hope of changing his behavior is through the aid of counseling. This especially applies to alcoholics, abusers, pathological liars, and other ingrained character flaws. Sometimes there is only a fine line which distinguishes these very serious behaviors from others less severe. However, a woman must follow her instincts and not remain in denial when faced with abusive behavior of any degree. If she remains in a relationship, suffering constant abuse, and doesn't seek help, she will eventually lose so much self-esteem that she'll be unable to make the necessary choices to help herself.

HOW TO GET **HIM** INTO COUNSELING

Most men will resist counseling. If he's acting unreasonably about many issues, don't expect him to be reasonable about seeing a counselor. So how do you get him to go? The method you utilize depends upon the severity of the dysfunction and the extent of the denial the person is in. Here are some options:

1. Offer A Compromise: Tell your spouse that if he agrees to counseling, then you will do something he wants. It could be to quit nagging, or make an effort to improve your sex life, or whatever you feel is an appropriate conciliation for the situation.

2. Warn Him About The Effects Of His Behavior: Tell him you may not resort to divorce, but the marriage is going to suffer to the extent that you'll both be miserable without professional help.

3. Recruit A Third Party: With very resistant spouses, enlist the help of an authority figure your husband respects and trusts. It might be his father, his brother, a clergyman, or his best friend. This person will help you try to convince your spouse that... A. he needs to change his thinking and attitude about a specific problem; and B. it will require counseling to do it.

4. Issue An Ultimatum: Tell your spouse that if he doesn't get help, then the marriage is over. And be prepared to back it up if he calls your bluff by having taken one or more of the following actions appropriate to your situation:

  a. you have consulted an attorney about your legal rights should you decide to separate

  b. you have informed his family about your intentions and have their support

  c. you have discussed the situation with the children and have their support and understanding

5. Plan An Intervention: This is a much more "aggressive" approach and is utilized when most other methods fail. It is accomplished by gathering the offender's family and friends together where they "confront" him directly, armed with the facts of why he needs professional help. They should show concern and caring but more importantly, be brutally blunt in their assessment of his dysfunctional behavior. In theory, this approach will leave him with no other option but to accept the fact that everyone he cares about feels that he is in dire need of professional help. And in most cases, the experience is powerful enough to motivate him to get help immediately.

Every relationship will endure hundreds of problems over the years. But it's the denial, lack of compromise, and unwillingness to seek help which are the real dangers to the relationship. And no matter how you arrive at a solution, it's vital that you do SOMETHING. Identifying the REAL issues and working towards a compromise whenever possible will help bring about a successful resolution to any problem.

ABOUT THE AUTHOR

"Why Men Don't Have A Clue" is the tenth book written by national best sell-ing author Jan King. She holds a B.A. in Education from the University of Connecticut and an M.A. in Education from the University of Pennsylvania. As a relationship expert, she is frequently invited as a guest on national TV talk shows including *Geraldo, Ricki Lake, Donahue, Jenny Jones, Montel Williams, Rolanda, Jerry Springer,* and *Judge For Yourself.*

She is happily married, the mother of two college-aged sons, and resides in Los Angeles.

TITLES BY CCC PUBLICATIONS

RETAIL $4.99

CAN SEX IMPROVE YOUR GOLF?
THE COMPLETE BOOGER BOOK
THINGS YOU CAN DO WITH A USELESS MAN
FLYING FUNNIES
MARITAL BLISS & OTHER OXYMORONS
THE VERY VERY SEXY ADULT DOT-TO-DOT BOOK
THE DEFINITIVE FART BOOK
THE COMPLETE WIMP'S GUIDE TO SEX
THE CAT OWNER'S SHAPE UP MANUAL
PMS CRAZED: TOUCH ME AND I'LL KILL YOU!
RETIRED: LET THE GAMES BEGIN
MALE BASHING: WOMEN'S FAVORITE PASTIME
THE OFFICE FROM HELL
FOOD & SEX
FITNESS FANATICS
YOUNGER MEN ARE BETTER THAN RETIN-A
BUT OSSIFER, IT'S NOT MY FAULT

RETAIL $4.95

1001 WAYS TO PROCRASTINATE
THE WORLD'S GREATEST PUT-DOWN LINES
HORMONES FROM HELL II
SHARING THE ROAD WITH IDIOTS
THE GREATEST ANSWERING MACHINE MESSAGES OF ALL TIME
WHAT DO WE DO NOW?? (A Guide For New Parents)
HOW TO TALK YOUR WAY OUT OF A TRAFFIC TICKET
THE BOTTOM HALF (How To Spot Incompetent Professionals)
LIFE'S MOST EMBARRASSING MOMENTS
HOW TO ENTERTAIN PEOPLE YOU HATE
YOUR GUIDE TO CORPORATE SURVIVAL
THE SUPERIOR PERSON'S GUIDE TO EVERYDAY IRRITATIONS
GIFTING RIGHT

RETAIL $5.95
50 WAYS TO HUSTLE YOUR FRIENDS ($5.99)
HORMONES FROM HELL
HUSBANDS FROM HELL
KILLER BRAS & Other Hazards Of The 50's
IT'S BETTER TO BE OVER THE HILL THAN UNDER IT
HOW TO REALLY PARTY!!!
WORK SUCKS
THE PEOPLE WATCHER'S FIELD GUIDE
THE UNOFFICIAL WOMEN'S DIVORCE GUIDE
THE ABSOLUTE LAST CHANCE DIET BOOK
FOR MEN ONLY (How To Survive Marriage)
THE UGLY TRUTH ABOUT MEN
NEVER A DULL CARD
RED HOT MONOGAMY (In Just 60 Seconds A Day) ($6.95)

RETAIL $3.95
YOU KNOW YOU'RE AN OLD FART WHEN...
NO HANG-UPS
NO HANG-UPS II
NO HANG-UPS III
GETTING EVEN WITH THE ANSWERING MACHINE
HOW TO SUCCEED IN SINGLES BARS
HOW TO GET EVEN WITH YOUR EXES
TOTALLY OUTRAGEOUS BUMPER-SNICKERS ($2.95)

NO HANG-UPS – CASSETTES   RETAIL $4.98
Vol. I: GENERAL MESSAGES (Female)
Vol. I: GENERAL MESSAGES (Male)
Vol. II: BUSINESS MESSAGES (Female)
Vol. II: BUSINESS MESSAGES (Male)
Vol. III: 'R' RATED MESSAGES (Female)
Vol. III: 'R' RATED MESSAGES (Male)
Vol. IV: SOUND EFFECTS ONLY
Vol. V: CELEBRI-TEASE

NOTES

NOTES

NOTES

NOTES